CW00821828

7 Steps to

Effective Public Speaking

Prem P. Bhalla

GOODWILL PUBLISHING HOUSE®

B-3 RATTAN JYOTI, 18 RAJENDRA PLACE
NEW DELHI-110008 (INDIA)

© Publishers

No part of this publication may be reproduced; stored in a retrieval system or transmitted in any form or by any means, mechanical, photocopying or otherwise without the prior written permission of the publisher.

Published by
GOODWILL PUBLISHING HOUSE®
B-3 Rattan Jyoti, 18 Rajendra Place
New Delhi-110008 (INDIA)
Tel. : 25750801, 25820556
Fax : 91-11-25764396
e-mail : goodwillpub@vsnl.net
website : www.goodwillpublishinghouse.com

Printed at Rajiv Book Binding House, Delhi

Contents

Preface

Step 1. Speaking in public   1

Step 2. Essentials of public speaking   23

Step 3. Developing speaking skills   47

Step 4. Making the speech effective   70

Step 5. Pitfalls to avoid   93

Step 6. Aids to speaking   113

Step 7. Towards greater perfection   134

Preface

The ability to speak effectively to a group of people can add a new dimension to a person's life. Unfortunately, most people are in the grip of a strong fear of speaking in public. This restraints them from developing speaking skills. These people live under the impression that speaking skills are inherited, that they are a gift of God. It is not so. Every person can acquire speaking skills, and with practice and experience go on to become an effective speaker.

The lack of good speaking skills has encouraged mediocrity even amongst the most capable business and professional personnel. This has further resulted in restricted development of individuals, businesses and professions. People are compelled to accept mediocrity as a standard of behaviour.

Effective public speakers are a result of good training, and not because of special talents inherited from the parents. However, it is true that just as children of parents who can communicate well become good communicators, the children of parents who possess good speaking skills learn them sooner than the others.

Public speaking skills were a part of the teaching curriculum over 2000 years ago. Despite political upheavals and changes, even today there is a great need for people who can speak well at the workplace and in the community. The emphasis given to this area of learning is insufficient at school and college level. Most people strive to acquire these skills much later when they feel the lack of it in later life.

This book aims at taking you step by step into the intricacies of speaking well before a group of people or a larger audience. It will help you understand the essentials of public speaking. It will also guide you to develop speaking skills for use in everyday life. Through determination and perseverance, you can develop speaking skills that can be used at the workplace and in the community.

— **Prem P. Bhalla**

Speaking in Public

Progressive individuals aspiring for top positions in business and professions are aware of the need to be able to speak in public. Many begin to acquire the skills when still at school by participating in elocution contests and debates. Others begin to appreciate the importance when in college, or when seeking admission to a career-oriented course. A few opt to acquire the skills much later when they look at it as a deficiency in the skills that they possess.

Many persons become eager to acquire speaking skills only when they realise that they can rise much higher in the workplace and the society with these skills. Almost in every sphere of life one needs to talk to groups of people — in housing societies, at the workplace, in clubs and organisations. In government positions this skill is particularly helpful. Speaking skills help a person to communicate better. Both men and women need this skill. For every proficient person, this is the first step to leadership positions.

A person who can speak well is an asset to every workplace. Effective communication plays a significant role in all business and professional positions. With greater competition at all levels, the importance of

1

speaking skills is assuming still greater attention. In-house training has become the need of the hour, and public speaking skills prove useful for the purpose. The ability to speak effectively helps in becoming a better teacher, and at the workplace it helps to become a better leader.

PUBLIC SPEAKING SKILLS

The need for public speaking skills is not of recent origin. It dates back to thousands of years. It is said that the first textbook on the subject was written over 2000 years ago. It was based upon the practices followed and the experience gained by the Greek orators. The Latins copied and modified the art of public speaking. At that time, public speaking was taught and formed a part of public and private life.

History confirms that public speaking skills can move millions of people both in positive and negative directions. While positive guidance by leaders has helped to stop wars and build nations, negative use of the speaking ability has created hatred, and has been the cause of conflicts, wars and loss to life and property.

The development of parliamentary system of governance gave rise to political orators. The ability to speak persuasively helped to win the confidence of the citizens. We see this happening in all democratic nations today.

It cannot be overlooked that public speaking can flourish only in a society where the citizens enjoy the freedom of speech. Public speaking can be learnt and developed only through eloquence and debate. When the society is subdued, a person cannot express views freely.

In such circumstances, the development of public speaking skills is not for the average citizen.

In the modern times, the average citizen is receiving information from many sources — the newspapers, magazines, books, radio, television news, etc. The revolution in Information Technology has further added to the quantum of information. Internet has linked people and knowledge all over the world. This has added to the confusion in the minds of people. The average person appreciates the information that is available to him or her, but at the same time it is difficult for a person to differentiate between plain information and what is useful.

Public speaking has an important role to dispel the confusion in the minds of people. In every sphere of life, there is a lot of information. To put this information to use, it is necessary that knowledgeable speakers help people differentiate what is useful information, and what isn't.

Think it over…

There is no power like that of true oratory. Caesar controlled men by exciting their fears; Cicero by captivating their affections and swaying their passions. The influence of the one perished with its author; that of the other continues to this day.

— *Henry Clay*

SPEAKING AT THE WORKPLACE

The ability to speak to groups of people is an essential skill for persons who desire to pursue one of the many modern careers. Unfortunately, public speaking, as a skill, is not taught in the conventional schools and colleges. Only opportunities are provided for the children to participate in elocution contests and debates as a part of teaching the spoken language. At college level, debates and other similar activities are limited to institutions offering courses in conventional subjects. In technical institutions the emphasis is on seminars and workshops, and speaking is restricted to the specialised subjects only.

Teaching

Of all professions teachers need to speak the most. If a teacher cannot communicate well through spoken words, the person has no right to be a teacher. Teaching requires a very high level of communication ability. As a profession, teaching provides livelihood to a very large number of men and women at all levels. This is a worldwide picture. The skills and abilities required at different levels vary greatly. Teachers at the primary level perform better with an instinctive understanding of little children, who respond to rhythm and rhyme, and the teachers teach them through poems, music and singing.

Grown up children and college going youth have different needs of learning. They respond better to teachers who can express themselves well, and logically carry forward the process of teaching new subjects. The teachers must have communication skills that fulfil this need.

Teaching is no longer limited to school and college going young people only. Working adults need to update their knowledge in their subject of specialisation periodically. This has necessitated larger companies to have human resource development departments that conduct refresher courses for the personnel. The smaller companies avail the facilities of consultants who specialise in adult professional education at the workplace. They conduct seminars to suit the needs of the clients. Every company needs efficient personnel.

Medicine

Medicine is a major professional activity in the society. The communication between a doctor and the patients is restricted to one-to-one conversation. The need for public speaking in this field is restricted to speaking at professional seminars, workshops and conferences.

Law

The written and the spoken word is the backbone of the legal profession. While it is important that legal documents must be well drafted, a professional in the field of law needs to be equally well equipped with speaking skills. Speaking skills draw immediate attention when one hears lawyers argue a case before a judge in the courtroom. Voices go up and down, sometimes in rhythm, and at another time to shock, to highlight salient features of the point of dispute. Words are carefully chosen and used to convince the judge. Oratorical skills help the lawyer to score while others just watch as mute spectators.

Engineering and Technology

The field of engineering and technology leads one to factories and homes. The success of this vast field depends entirely upon communication skills, both written and verbal. If it were not for these skills and abilities, human development would have come to a standstill long ago.

Speaking skills are used to exchange the growing knowledge in this field through seminars and training programmes. They are also used to motivate the workforce.

Selling

Who has not seen a salesperson speaking emotionally to convince prospective customers? Selling requires excellent speaking skills. Many of the presentations are one-to-one between the salesman and the prospective customers, but it is equally important for the salesman to be able to make presentations before a group of people. Selling is one of the most competitive professions. Besides the presentations to prospective customers, one needs good speaking skills to motivate and keep the vast sales force that go out in the field to sell at a high level of enthusiasm.

The Business Office

In any business office the need for good communication skills cannot be overlooked. The typical office is a hub of communication activity. Letters are coming and going, inter-office memos are being exchanged, reports are prepared, presentations are perfected and presented, and a variety of meetings are conducted. Every activity is linked with the ability to communicate. What is the staff doing? They are trying to sell themselves and their products. In any routine job complacency is bound to creep in. This causes the spirits to sag. Therefore, a major need in every office is to keep the personnel motivated to keep performing. Public speaking skills help the management to fulfil this need.

Think it over…

I do not believe that one should speak unless, deep down in his heart, he feels convinced that he has a message to deliver.

— *Booker T. Washington*

MEETINGS AND ASSEMBLIES

Millions of meetings are organised every day at places of work and in the society. Unfortunately, a vast majority fails because of poor communication skills. A large sum of money is lost each day because of these meetings. Good meetings are dependent upon organisational and speaking skills. If every participant in a meeting possesses good speaking skills, every meeting would be successful.

An assembly is much larger than the usual meetings. Speakers address a comparatively larger audience on different subjects. The success of these assemblies depends entirely upon the skills of the speakers assigned to address the audience.

SYMPOSIUMS AND SEMINARS

A symposium is a conference or meeting to discuss a particular subject. The word: symposium has a Greek origin. At that time it referred to a party where people got together to discuss, debate or talk about themselves. In the present context, a symposium is an academic meeting, where different speakers put forth their views to an audience of learned people.

A seminar is a meeting where a discussion leader facilitates the teaching of the students in one or more groups. The emphasis is on interactive discussion, leading to a better understanding of the subject. A seminar may be organised by a university, or a commercial or professional organisation. It is usual to discuss assignments, and question and debate on specific issues. The atmosphere is normally informal.

While symposiums and seminars promote knowledge, an important aspect is for the speakers to have the ability to convincingly put forth their thoughts and ideas. Without the ability to speak effectively, not much can be gained. For this reason, even the academicians feel that they need to possess good speaking skills.

ACADEMIC CONFERENCE

An academic conference differs from a symposium in that it may not be for academicians. Generally, an academic conference is for researchers, who may get together to exchange information amongst each other. If the audience were large, it would be called a conference. With few participants it would be called a workshop.

Information is generally provided through concise presentations of 10 to 30 minutes duration. This includes the time for discussion. Copies of the presentation may be distributed to the participants, or may be included as part of the conference proceedings bound together and a copy given to each delegate.

The delegates who desire to make a presentation are usually requested to submit a write-up of the presentation in advance. The organising committee reviews this and, on finding it suitable, includes it in the conference programme. Since most of the presentations are written in advance, they are usually read to the audience. Presentations on scientific subjects are supported by visuals on a laptop computer.

At any academic conference only those presentations will be remembered, or create an effective impact, when the presentation is made by a person possessing good speaking skills.

CONVENTIONS

When a meeting or a conference is very large, it is called a convention. Like all other meetings a convention is held at a place, time and date that are fixed earlier. It aims at discussing subjects of common interest by delegates and representatives. Since the participation is large, and the deliberations restricted to only a few, to keep everyone involved, it is usual to include entertainment features during the convention.

Many organisations are made up of smaller units, as we notice unions, chapters, and clubs like Rotary and Lions, and conventions are the annual get-togethers of these organisations. Opportunity is provided to the smaller units to send representatives or delegates to express their opinions on various subjects. Conventions are known to feature the best of public speakers, which are given wide publicity in advance.

One can see some of the finest presentations by eminent speakers at a convention. One can learn a lot on public speaking on these occasions.

SPEAKING SKILLS IN OTHER PLACES

Besides meetings and assemblies, seminars and

symposiums, academic conferences and conventions, speaking skills are very useful in many other places.

Few people notice it critically, and without being aware of it, we hear radio jockeys speaking on the radio every day. A radio jockey is a person who hosts a radio talk show. The skills used are not the same that are used by public speakers, but there is great similarity in that a radio jockey needs to have a good control over the voice, must know the language well and be swift in response to some of the listeners who interact on the show. However, a radio jockey does not face the audience and works from the broadcasting studio. A radio newsreader also needs to have good voice quality and pronunciation.

A television host or anchor also needs good voice quality and speaking skills. The host is clearly visible on the screen and needs to project a positive image through facial expressions and body language. The host interacts with the audience on the show and is always in the view of the camera. At times the host also talks directly to the audience watching the television show and faces the camera straight.

Newsreaders on television channels may broadcast the news sitting at the desk, but sometimes they do it standing, appearing to be talking extempore. News reporters speak directly from the spot where the news emerges. Since they are in direct view of the public amidst whom they stand and report, and are also being watched by millions of people viewing television, the news reporters need to have a control over their words, questions and statements that could become debatable in the event of a slip. Good speaking skills are an asset to every news reporter.

A disc jockey is a person who selects and plays pre-recorded music for an audience. The audience could be at a party, club, disco, or even huge stadium. The disc jockey may also speak, sing, propose toasts and give comments over prerecorded music discs. He may interact with the dancing audience, adding to the fun. He controls the music system simultaneously. The better the disc jockey's speaking skills, more the fun the audience enjoys.

A host at a live music show in a restaurant, club, auditorium or even a stadium needs to possess good speaking skills. He is the person who keeps the audience attracted and involved while performers come and go. He is truly the person who keeps the show moving and alive.

The word: host is popularly changed to Master of Ceremonies when the occasion is a public or private stage event. Master of Ceremonies is often abbreviated to MC, and sometimes spelt *emcee*. The MC presents the speakers, performers and keeps the event moving with occasional remarks, quips and comments.

The term Master of Ceremonies has its origin in the Catholic Church, where, as an official of the Papal Court, he is responsible for the conduct of the elaborate rituals pertaining to the Pope and the Sacred Liturgy.

Out of necessity the MC needs to possess good public speaking skills backed by a good knowledge of protocol and the speakers and performers to be presented to the audience. He needs to be gentle and yet firm to maintain discipline amongst the audience during the event.

A RUNNING COMMENTARY

In yet another field where one can observe speaking skills, though of a different kind, is at the running commentary given at games like cricket, football, hockey, tennis, field games and others. Live television has made it possible to have visuals and the commentary simultaneously, making it easier to have a first hand report of the game, just as though one were occupying a special seat.

A good commentator needs to have good speaking skills and also a good knowledge of the game. Most commentators are retired players who have experienced the game first hand. Since the game is likely to extend over prolonged periods, the responsibility of giving the commentary is shared by a team of commentators, all knowledgeable about the game, but fluent in different languages like English and Hindi.

Besides the games, it is not unusual to have running commentaries about special occasions and events like the Republic Day Parade, or the Independence Day Celebrations. It is also not unusual to have running commentaries about celebration of festivals like the burning of Ravan's effigy at Dashera, or the immersion of the idols of Durga after Durga Puja, or of Sri Ganesh after Ganesh Chaturthi. Once again, it is good public speaking skills and knowledge of the event that make an effective commentary possible.

Think it over…

He is the eloquent man who can treat subjects of a humble nature with delicacy, lofty things impressively, and moderate things temperately.

— *Cicero*

LACK OF PUBLIC SPEAKING SKILLS

Despite the widespread need and use of public speaking skills in diverse fields of activity that touch every person in everyday life, it is surprising that very few people possess good public speaking skills. In the foregoing paragraphs we have seen how millions of people are touched every day with speaking skills in one form or another. However, only a few people are involved and use speaking skills to reach the millions through mass communication media.

In many of the fields discussed in the foregoing paragraphs speaking skills are used. However, many of these require a very different application as compared to public speaking. Radio jockeys, disc jockeys, newsreaders and television hosts are provided with written scripts, hidden computer screens and Teleprompters to guide and carry them through the show. In most cases, the persons are not in direct contact with the audience. It is only in live shows, performances and meetings that the host or the MC comes in contact with the audience.

At the grass-root level very few people acquire or use speaking skills effectively. We see it everyday at the workplace and in community life. Most people shy away from them. They rationalize the limitation by pretending to do well without the skills.

It is believed, and experience has proved it that wherever there is a shortage, the laws of supply and demand soon fill it up. However, public speaking skills are an exception. The fear of speaking before a group of people holds people back from acquiring the skills. This fear is rated next in importance only to the fear of death. Some confess to go a step further. They would rather be dead than to go through the fearful experience of speaking in public.

Appreciating the importance of effective communication children are taught in school how to read audibly, learn correct pronunciation of words, and be able to express themselves through speech. Elocution contests and debates are organised to encourage young people to acquire speaking skills. Only a few opt for these. The majority prefers to use their energies in other activities because of their fear of speaking in public. Even those who participate in speaking activities do so only as an extra curricular activity. The importance of speaking skills at the workplace is usually appreciated late in life.

A FLOOD OF INFORMATION

An important function of public speaking is to inform. But is the average citizen not already buried under information that is being hurled towards him or her from all directions? The newspapers, magazines, journals and books provide an untold amount of information. Almost all the radio and television channels broadcast news, live shows, talk shows, soaps and a variety of other programmes to cater to the tastes of children, teenagers, adults and senior citizens. The programmes inform, guide, teach and entertain. Unfortunately, much of the information is contradictory. It leaves the audience confused, concerned and worried. Only a few can appreciate what is right or wrong.

Mass communication of information through the press and electronic media does not readily help the individual. Everyone is different. The problems of every individual are unique. Every person is sensitive towards them. Information may help inform the enormity of the situation, but it cannot solve the particular problems. It would be far better if the problems could be tackled in smaller groups where individual speakers who are knowledgeable in their fields could speak and interact with the audience to help them live better. This way the right information could reach the right people at the right time.

SPEAKING SKILLS ARE ACQUIRED SKILLS

Contrary to what the majority of people believe speaking skills are acquired skills. They can be learned like any other skill. In ancient Greece public speaking formed a part of the teaching curriculum. With time and circumstances the priorities changed. Political changes had their own agenda. The needs of governance are not without their influence.

The aspiring young people must understand that dynamic public speakers are not born with special abilities. They acquire these through training and effort. After the basics have been learned the skills are further developed through practice. This is one field where a person can never say that he or she has had enough practice. Every opportunity to speak presents new challenges. The audience is different. The circumstances are also different. At every opportunity there is something to add to one's experience. The benefits that accrue become visible much later.

Speaking skills are an important element of leadership skills. A good leader needs to communicate effectively with the team and the public. In leadership roles, speaking skills are more important than writing skills. We all know how some of the greatest leaders of all time have changed the destinies of nations and the citizens through use of powerful public speaking. Strangely, not one of them was a born speaker. They learned the skill through study and effort.

Think it over...

It is the first rule in oratory that a man must first appear such as he would persuade others to be; and that can be accomplished only by the force of his life.

— *Swift*

LEARNING SPEAKING SKILLS

With the great shortage of effective speakers, does it mean that the people are just not interested in this field? No. With the great demand of good speakers who can effectively convey a message, many private institutions that provide studies in languages and personality development include public speaking as a part of the curriculum. In the short time that is available some speaking techniques are shared with the students. It is for them to develop these skills through practice. Information on public speaking is also available on the Internet. Interactive courses for study are also available. It is for the individual to gauge personal needs and work towards their fulfilment through study and practice.

Public speaking skills are in great demand in every field of activity. No business or professional organisation wants to be left behind. Since it is the workforce that takes an organisation towards their goal, the management is eager that the workforce must sharpen their management skills, teamwork, time management and communication skills, and most of all the ability to speak effectively to the workforce. Larger organisations have set up training facilities, but the smaller organisations are taking advantage of professional training organisations.

THE ABILITY TO PERSUADE

A public speaker speaks to inform, influence or entertain an audience. The most desirable element of public speaking is the ability to influence, or persuade the audience to act. This is not as simple as it sounds. The process depends upon four distinct components. The first is a person who speaks. Next, there has to be an appropriate message, which must be in a form and language that both the speaker and the audience can understand. Third, the audience must be receptive to the message. Finally, the reaction of the audience decides the effectiveness of the message.

An effective public speaker learns to use words that influence people. The speaker weaves the words into sentences and paragraphs that inform, touch and compel the audience to react. The speaker uses anecdotes, stories and humour to persuade and motivate the audience. The speaker's knowledge, confidence and abilities add strength to the presentation. Above all else, an effective speaker is known to understand human behaviour. It is with this knowledge that the speaker ultimately touches upon the emotions of the audience, and makes them act in a positive or negative direction.

ALL SPEAKERS ARE DIFFERENT

All speakers necessarily need to be learned and knowledgeable about what they speak. Without that they will not have a message to convey to the audience. Even when two persons speak on the same subject, one person may be more effective than the other in conveying the message to the audience. Why is it so? Both speakers possess different speaking skills. Considering that both are knowledgeable and prepared, a quality that separates one speaker from the other is the level of personal sincerity with which one speaks. While both will provide information and knowledge, one may go a step ahead to ensure that the knowledge being provided is of immediate use to the audience.

To be successful in any field, it is important that a person must provide a little more than what is expected from him or her. For example, a doctor normally treats a patient, but when he tells the patient how to remain healthy, he is providing extra service. In the same way, a lawyer represents the client in a court of law, but when he helps the client to prevent unnecessary litigation, he is providing extra service. A teacher would normally teach his subject to the class. However, those teachers are better remembered who teach values and guide the students to success. In the same way, speakers who are especially thoughtful about the needs of the audience are always appreciated.

Another remarkable quality in effective speakers is their ability to think differently from others. Two speakers speaking on the same subject would have the same things to talk about, but both will put it in different ways. The speaker who can interpret the same thing in many ways, and also explain how to differentiate between the right and wrong will eventually prove to be more effective. Success comes from doing the same thing differently. A speaker who is creative, innovative and thinks differently will definitely score over others. The audience loves novelty. They seek new ideas from speakers.

Speakers are also different in that each one is likely to use different techniques to elaborate upon the basic subject. Some will illustrate examples from their own lives, others will tell anecdotes and stories that help draw conclusions. Some will ask questions for which the audience has no answers, and then the speaker will go on to explain and answer the questions logically. Many use tales and fables. Some more entertain through humour and subtle remarks, and gradually lead to a conclusion. Many use their knowledge and humility to drive home the truth to the audience. Irrespective of the techniques speakers use, the important thing is to be effective in conveying the message to the audience.

The first lesson for an aspiring speaker should be to not copy any particular speaker's style, but rather learn the basics of public speaking, and gradually develop a personal style that would stand out.

Think it over...

An orator or author is never successful till he has learned to make his words smaller than his ideas.

— *Emerson*

GROWING STEP BY STEP

No aspiring speaker became great overnight. There are sportsmen, actors, singers and performers who may achieve great prominence overnight, but not public speakers. For them it is a long arduous journey. Though difficult, it is a very satisfying experience that one is useful to many people. Recognition is slow to come. It builds up gradually from one assignment to another.

Every effective public speaker started in a small way. Success comes in small measures, a little at each step. With each success a person builds up emotionally through added confidence, and physically through a better personality. One builds step by step.

Every aspiring speaker must begin by learning the basics of public speaking. None can do without them. Following the basics, at every step one must put in the best effort. Hard work shows. It will bring success. This success will build up into larger successes. Every person is bound to prepare in his or her own special way, and therefore, each person develops a style all of its own. It is this style that a person is known by in later years.

It does not matter whether a person is to speak to 5 people, or to 50 or even 500, what matters is how well prepared the speaker is to convey a valid message to the audience. If the message and the audience are right, the speaker is bound to succeed. The audience will talk about the presentation. When they talk, they will think about it. And when the thought process begins, sooner or later the audience will react through appropriate action.

Every speech builds up the speaker. A good public speaker is not restricted within the limits of one's field of specialisation. A good speaker looks at life from a much larger perspective as it touches everyone. To be able to speak well means to know humanity well. It means to know their hopes, concerns and aspirations. The knowledge helps one to live a better life, and also recommend and share it with the audience at every presentation.

POINTS TO PONDER

1. The importance of public speaking can be appreciated when we note that the first book on the subject was written more than 2000 years ago.

2. Without public speaking skills most people are not able to develop to their full potential at the workplace.

3. A very large number of meetings fail because of poor organisational and speaking skills.

4. The success of symposiums, seminars, workshops, conferences and conventions depend upon good speaking skills.

5. Radio jockeys, disc jockeys, MCs and commentators need good speaking skills.

6. There will always be shortage of good speakers.

7. Good public speakers help the audience to differentiate between information that is useful, and that which is not.

8. Everyone can acquire speaking skills.

9. Good speaking skills are required to persuade people to act.

10. Public speakers use different methods and techniques to achieve their purpose.

11. A person grows slowly in the field of public speaking.

Essentials of Public Speaking

Many people can be seen speaking in public. They are not necessarily public speakers. They speak because of the necessity to speak on account of their professional and business commitments. Some of them make additional effort to develop speaking skills, and emerge as effective public speakers. This immediately brings them to the notice of the senior management, or the people who matter. On the basis of speaking skills and abilities they are rated on a higher scale as compared to others.

Public speaking is a deliberate, structured method to inform, persuade or influence, and sometimes entertain a group of people. Besides communicating information to the audience, public speaking aims at persuading or motivating people. The ability to speak well to groups of people is a valuable skill.

What are the basic essentials that help promote good speaking skills? If the average person can understand the value of these basic qualities, and can cultivate them over a period of time, we would have many more effective public speakers.

A person is not born with public speaking skills. These skills are acquired gradually through learning. Even when we see the son or daughter of a good public speaker speaking well, it does not mean that the ability is inherited from one of the parents. The skill is learnt through observation and learning. There can be no better opportunity than to have a parent who can be a role model to inspire effective speaking skills, but a personal effort would still be necessary.

SELF-CONFIDENCE

The first essential of becoming a good public speaker is self-confidence. Observe any person standing to speak in public. You cannot overlook the confidence of the person — the way he or she stands, smiles, looks at the audience to establish eye contact, and then begins to speak in clear, straightforward words that appear to emerge from the heart.

Self-confidence comes slowly. It is dependent on many other qualities that have to be acquired gradually, as one goes through school and college. Every individual is exposed to two kinds of influences — positive and negative. The positive influences include a caring and loving temperament, belief in truthfulness and honesty, and being thoughtful about everyone. These qualities help to build a positive personality. This shows as self-confidence.

When a person is selfish, greedy and jealous, and easily gives in to anger, the negative reactions also influence the individual. This ultimately results in lack of confidence. When negative persons appear confident, it is only an assumed form of confidence. It is not long before the truth comes to the surface. Many people entertain negative thoughts about their appearance and physique, others because of their family background. Many more fail because they are unable to forget a not-too-pleasant past. To succeed, these insignificant thoughts must be overcome. With the control of thoughts, feelings and actions, one is able to adopt a positive attitude. This way self-confidence begins to grow.

Self-confidence emerges from success. In itself each success is very small. When it accumulates one-by-one, the effect adds to emerge as self-confidence. Can you imagine a newborn child walking? Of course, you cannot. That would be against nature. The child must first learn to sit, then crawl and eventually learn to stand up and start walking. The walking can later be transformed to running, and eventually even to sprinting. Self-confidence emerges the same way, step by step, one little success followed by yet another success. Public speaking skills are gradually built upon the foundation of self-confidence.

Life is dynamic. Continuous change is a characteristic of life. With effort, skills and abilities will grow, and also the self-confidence. One must concentrate on activities in which success has been achieved earlier. At the same time, one must keep learning new things. The added knowledge and the power that accompanies it, helps strengthen self-confidence. Try a hand at new activities. Success is the best confidence builder. Keep repeating your successes. At no time should your faith in your personal ability suffer. Increase your interests. Go out where you can meet new people and learn new things. With new successes, your self-confidence will grow.

Think it over...

Confidence, in conversation, has a greater share than wit.

— *Rochefoucauld*

YOUR PERSONALITY

How do you rate yourself as a person? Are you attractive? Do people give you a second glance when you enter a room? Are you content with your appearance? Your physique? Health? The way you carry yourself? Unless you rate yourself high, you cannot expect others to do so. Unless you believe that you are attractive, you will not attract anyone.

To be attractive, one must learn to understand the ways of nature. Nature has made everyone and everything beautiful. If we are not satisfied with what nature has made us, it is our own fault. We meddle with its ways even though its demands are few and simple. We must learn to be in harmony with nature.

Good health is essential for a charming personality. A good physique does not necessarily mean one is healthy. Only when a person enjoys physical and emotional well-being can one be described healthy. If you are weak in a particular area, it should not discourage you. You should instead learn to live with limitations. Nature has spared no pains to make the human body perfect. Only when we burden it with a load that is heavier than what the body can bear comfortably, stress begins to affect the weaker areas, robbing the person of vitality. One must learn to live at a pace that is in harmony with the health and personal abilities.

To be healthy and attractive, the body requires that the nutritive requirements must be provided. The needs are varied. All of them must be provided to the body. Milk, fruits, nuts and vegetables are rich sources of the vital substances that affect the skin, hair, eyes, etc. They must form a part of the daily diet.

Personal attractiveness also depends upon posture and carriage. Good manners and etiquette are never overlooked. One is always attracted to a person who smiles effortlessly, and speaks convincingly. A person who has his back hunched, stands leaning against walls and furniture, and walks uneasily cannot be called attractive. The way a person sits, stands, walks, greets and meets people decides how attractive he or she is to them.

Clothes speak loudly of an individual. The way a person dresses can help draw immediate attention. The elegance of dress does not necessarily come from expensive clothes. Clean, crisp clothes worn without much fuss always enhance personal charm. Everybody appreciates cleanliness and simplicity.

The face is always the centre of attraction. The power to attract comes from the thoughts. The greater the influence one has on the thoughts, the better are the chances of developing personal magnetism. Just as happiness and gaiety attract goodwill and well-being, feelings of anxiety, worry, anger and envy leave their telltale marks on the face. A person must learn to be happy to radiate the inner beauty of the self.

KNOWLEDGE OF THE LANGUAGE

One cannot communicate information or ideas without knowing the language, which the audience can understand. Those who travel frequently know how important it is to speak the language of the area they visit. Any effort to speak would be futile unless you know and speak the language the people can understand. Even within India, where as many as 22 languages are recognised, sometimes it becomes difficult to speak to people. Hindi and English are the usual link languages. Many times the people may not be acquainted with either of these languages.

In Europe, the ability to speak English is useful, but sometimes one is unable to communicate without the knowledge of French and German.

Besides the knowledge of the language, it is essential that the speaker must choose words that carry the message effectively. The choice of the words is not easy. Any writer would confirm it. Many people shy away from writing a simple letter because of the fear of choosing the wrong words. Choosing words is easier when writing because you can take your time to put it on paper.

While speaking, the choice of words can be difficult unless one has a good vocabulary of the particular language. The words must flow. The listener can become impatient if there are gaps in the speech. He or she may get irritated, and the verbal communication can fail completely. Every public speaker has faced such situations. One must speak fluently. To be effective, one must be armed with the appropriate words, and leave the rest to the audience.

BODY LANGUAGE

Have you ever observed that people are communicating something or the other through body language all the time? Would it not be useful if individuals could understand and give a meaning to these messages? These messages come in the form of body gestures. They could convey both positive and negative feelings. The positive feelings are visible as enthusiasm, joy and happiness. The negative feelings are seen as boredom, irritation and loneliness, and also as anger and frustration.

Observe how children behave at school. Observe how they talk to each other. Observe how they greet teachers or parents visiting the school. Observe their reactions to different situations. Try to figure out how they feel. Why do they behave as they do? You will gradually begin to understand body language.

Analysis follows observation. Try to analyse what you have observed. One can conclude little on the basis of a single body movement or gesture. It has been observed that gestures come in groups. These gestures are linked with personal attitudes. For example, if a person is nervous, the face may turn pale, the hands may tremble and there may be sweat on the brows. In the same way, if a person is exposed to a ghastly scene, the person may close the eyes tightly and cover the mouth with the hand to stifle a shriek.

On observing gestures a person can give meaning to each gesture and then analyse the group as a whole. Accurate evaluation cannot be learnt overnight. One needs to persevere through hits and misses. The observation becomes keen with some effort. With some thought, the evaluation too becomes accurate. One must be patient while analysing the gestures. A hasty reaction could be misleading. It is better to think, consider motives and possible reactions, and then react. This way the body language can become an important element for the speaker to make the communication effective.

When observing body language, a person must be able to differentiate between voluntary and involuntary gestures. In learning body language one observes reactions to particular situations. Normally, these reactions are involuntary. They happen without the person being aware of them. Taking a cue from them, the other people respond.

All gestures may not be involuntary. Who has not seen a child pretending to have a stomachache to avoid going to school? His gestures compel the mother to think twice before compelling him to go. Who has not seen an employee laugh at a joke simply because it was narrated by his boss? Even in everyday life, using the knowledge of body language, people make voluntary gestures to mislead others.

A capable public speaker needs to understand body language, one's own and that of the audience. This is useful to building a rapport between the speaker and the audience, and to convey the message effectively.

Think it over...

"Knowledge, without commonsense", says Lee, "is folly; without method, it is a waste; without kindness, it is fanaticism; without religion, it is death." But with commonsense, it is wisdom; with method, it is power; with charity, it is beneficence; with religion, it is virtue, and life, and peace.

— *Farrar*

KNOWLEDGE AND WISDOM

To enjoy confidence in everyday life it is necessary that one must be knowledgeable and wise. Most people interpret having gone to school and college, to mean that they are knowledgeable. They might know whatever they have learnt at school and later at college, but the knowledge that one gains from these institutions is only a foundation for a career. Life is built on this foundation. However, additional knowledge gained through hands on working experience is required to build a strong superstructure.

Work experience is not limited only to the workplace. It pertains equally to the home and the society. One cannot live a secluded life. One needs to relate equally with people at home, the workplace and the society. True knowledge emerges from an individual's experience in different places and situations.

Younger people who possess academic knowledge pertaining to their field of learning and practice may be able to speak convincingly about their field of specialisation. That would amount to providing information and knowledge only. Such a presentation would lack the flavour of wisdom. Knowledge becomes wisdom only after it has been tried in everyday life. The experiences that follow need to be integrated with it. This way the knowledge gradually emerges as wisdom in that field of activity.

Public speaking aims at persuading the audience to accept new information and ideas. Therefore, it is necessary that to be effective the speaker must be knowledgeable. Practical experience is helpful. Since public speaking pertains to people, and as everyone is aware that human needs can be complicated, the greater the knowledge of the speaker, the better the opportunity to make the presentation effective.

BECOME AN EFFECTIVE LISTENER

Before one can learn to speak effectively, one must learn to be a good listener. This requires a person to understand how the listening process works. This is particularly important because when a person speaks, the knowledge about listening skills will help understand the response of the audience.

The process of listening can be divided into smaller segments. We can understand each segment step by step. It begins with the hearing of the message correctly. The next step is to interpret or understand what has been heard. Then the logical step is to evaluate the message, forming an opinion about it. Depending upon the use of the information to the listener, the next step is to store or memorise it for future use. The final step is to respond by acknowledging what has been heard and understood.

In a group when several people hear the same message, it is not necessary that all of them will respond in the same way to the message. Several factors influence the listening process. Noise may not permit a message to be heard correctly. When a person is bored, whatever is being heard may not sound attractive. In the same way, people who have mental blocks may not respond favourably to certain ideas. A restless person may interrupt the speaker and not get the correct message. Fatigue is also known to affect an individual's receptivity.

Listening effectively is an acquired skill. It requires one to concentrate on what is being said. Since the mind has the capacity to listen much faster than what is being spoken, the listener is tempted to interrupt, and to agree with, or contradict whatever is being spoken. To be a good listener, it is necessary that one must refrain from speaking until the other person has finished conveying the message.

To become a good listener one must sit straight with the back erect. This enhances attentiveness. The next step should be to establish an eye contact with the speaker. When a person looks at the speaker, there is an unsaid assurance that one is listening. Think of how the information that is being provided will be useful to you. If extraneous thoughts invade the mind, remind yourself that what is being said is important to you. When you are part of a group to whom information is being imparted, nodding the head confirms that you are listening. If possible, confirm what has been said.

Think it over...

Nature has given us two ears, two eyes, and but one tongue, to the end that we should hear and see more than we speak.

— *Socrates*

THE VOICE

The voice radiates personal charm. A person with a pleasant and rhythmic voice draws immediate attention. Have you noticed how a good speaker sways the audience as he or she paints pictures with words? The modulations of the voice are smooth and rhythmic. The speaker makes the audience laugh or cry. The audience sits still enamoured by the voice.

No speaker acquired these abilities at birth. Every orator learnt to speak, to attract and hold the attention of the audience. This is possible only through training and personal effort. The latent abilities need to be developed.

The voice is greatly influenced by the condition of the vocal cords, the throat and the lungs. Public speakers and singers take special care of their voice. They do deep breathing exercises to enhance lung capacity and control the voice. Nervous disorders also affect speech. This is common with people in the later stages of their life. Some of these problems can be corrected with medical care. One has to live with some conditions.

Poor hearing also affects speech quality. With impaired hearing, one is unable to appreciate the correct phonetics, and thereby the speech too is affected. Stammering and lisping are common problems that affect articulation. This could also be due to a cleft lip or palate, or to a nervous setback. Partial paralysis too affects the quality of speech. These are childhood problems and can be corrected with timely medical care.

Poor voice quality is a common cause for ineffective communication. The quality of the voice is an inherited factor. It can be trained for better performance. Cultural differences also influence the way words are pronounced. For example, within India, English pronunciation varies significantly from the north to the south, and from the east to the west. The differences are so marked that it is possible to identify the background of the person who is speaking. Even within the United Kingdom, the home of Queen's English, dialects differ from one area to another, sometimes making it difficult for an average person to understand what is being said.

The people migrating from developing nations to developed nations have taken with them peculiarities of grammar and pronunciation they use. With a large number of people using faulty words and phonetics, there is a major difference of opinion amongst language experts whether the changing words and their pronunciation must be accepted in the language. Those who are in favour of preserving the language in pure form insist that even though the speech has been corrupted, the written language must remain pure. Another group insists that the spoken language is the basis of the written language, and the changing words must be incorporated into the language. Only time will tell which way the wind blows.

Think it over...

The foundation of knowledge must be laid by reading. General principles must be had from books, which, however, must be brought to the test of real life.

— *Johnson*

SPEAKING

To speak means to say something, to communicate a message through the use of voice. This is possible with the use of the vocal cords and the vocal apparatus situated in the lower part of the neck in a human being.

The study of speech sounds is called phonetics. The study of phonetics is important because one's ability to communicate through the spoken word is greatly influenced by the quality of the sound, the tone and the rhythm, besides the information that is being communicated.

The tone of the voice refers to the musical effect with reference to the pitch, quality and strength of the voice expressing a feeling, emotion or mood. The pitch describes the extent of the sound or tone as high or low. The sound is said to be rhythmic when it follows a strong, regular and repeated musical pattern. This is of special significance when teaching little children to speak. They respond better to rhythmic, musical sounds.

In everyday life, the same words can influence the listener in different ways when the tone of the voice is altered. This fact is widely used in debates and declamation contests. Professionally, legal practitioners are known to use this technique to highlight certain facts, and underplay others, when arguing a case before the judge. Politicians use their knowledge of phonetics to influence the citizens when seeking their support. Good public speakers are equally well known to confidently present their point of view before large audiences to inform, educate or entertain many people through what they have to say.

Religious leaders and gurus are known to chant hymns, prayers, *mantras* and *slokas* to please God. At the same time they convey the message of happiness and bliss to the common man. All religious preachers, irrespective of the religion they practise or follow, use this technique. Millions of devotees are influenced by the use of words that touch their emotions. Such is the power of speech.

The use and influence of singing, rather than speaking, is well known not only to entertain people around the world, but also to arouse them emotionally. Devotional singing and music are used in almost every religion around the world. In the same way, singing and music are used to arouse patriotism in the hearts of people, and also motivate armed forces and security services to protect their motherland even at the cost of their lives.

THE READING HABIT

Reading is a basic necessity to gain knowledge. Unfortunately, most people are not fond of reading. Very few people are inclined to read the newspaper that they buy every day. The best they do is to look at the headlines on the front page, see if there are any interesting pictures, and then put aside the paper. The younger people reach for the sports page. Most businessmen take a quick look at the business section, the stock exchange section and the advertisements. The family shares the Sunday newspaper. The interest is very limited.

How many people read magazines? Very few, indeed! Some people read only when they travel because they have nothing to keep them occupied. Very few people are regular readers. In how many homes do we see books? Most people will agree that they haven't bought a book since they left college. To many people the purchase of a book is a luxury rather than a necessity. The book industry depends largely upon the textbook requirements in schools and colleges. The percentage of reading public is small.

All progress comes from the use of new knowledge. There can be no better way of acquiring knowledge than through books. If one does not want to be left behind in life, one must read, and read! There is no end to knowledge or to learning. The more you have of it, the more you want of it. Enjoy what you read. You will want more of it.

People have strange reading preferences. Most of them read cheap magazines. When they read the newspaper, they will read about cases of theft, housebreaking or rape reported. When they read magazines, they are on the lookout for gossip and scandals about film and political personalities. Even the books they read pertain to scandals and murders. The circulation of these publications speaks of their popularity.

People who desire to reach great heights cannot afford to read material of low value. With limited time available, reading has necessarily got to be purposeful. When reading, choose what appears important to you. A proper selection of reading material is essential. It is often said that you cannot judge a book by its cover. Do not be charmed by the cover. Read the blurb on the back cover. Check it with the contents. Browse through the book. If you find it will be useful, buy the book.

To improve reading efficiency, a person must read as many books and magazines as possible. The reading speed and assimilation are important. This is possible with a wide eye span. This way one can read several words at a time, appreciating key words, phrases and ideas. This is possible because one reads in thought groups instead of reading words. It is also necessary that one must read mentally, not through spoken words. Lip movements reduce reading speed. Whatever is read must be understood. One should assimilate what the author has written. It should not be confused with personal opinions and mental blocks. The subject must be given the importance it deserves.

LEARNING SPEAKING SKILLS

Learning the art of speaking is not new. It dates back to the times of Aristotle and Quintilian. Oratory has always been an important skill for use in private and public life. It was a part of the teaching curriculum in ancient Greece. Oratory has always been a great asset to the ministers in the courts of kings and monarchs. As the political scene changed and parliaments, legislative and other democratic agencies emerged, politicians have found public speaking skills useful to persuade the public and their colleagues alike.

To encourage eloquence in school children, they are taught elocution, the skill of clear and expressive speech. They are encouraged to recite poems and participate in declamation contests and debates to enhance their confidence and speaking skills.

Declamation refers to the act or art of speaking, or reciting, in a dramatic or passionate way. The subject of the speech is invariably not written by the child who is speaking. The important thing is to be able to speak clearly, and to control the pitch and the tone of the voice to persuade the listeners to hear and appreciate what is being said. It is common for teachers to select well-written speeches of famous people for children to practise speaking skills. Reciting of poems helps add rhythm and emotions to what is said.

The art of speaking well forms a part of learning languages in schools and colleges. Unfortunately, at that stage, it receives only a limited attention of the students. It is only later when young people join specific vocations where speaking skills are important that they join special classes and develop speaking skills. Many learn speaking skills through self-study and practice. It is interesting to observe that when a person is able to speak convincingly, he or she is accepted as intellectually superior. Such is the power of effective public speaking.

DEBATE

A step ahead of narration is the art of debate, which aims at a formal discussion, where opposing views are presented and argued. The purpose of the debate is to consider an appropriate action in a given situation.

Just like declamation contests, children are encouraged to participate in school debates, initially held at class level and later at inter-house level within the school. It is common to have inter-school debates amongst a group of schools. Later, there would be inter-college debates. This is useful training to the students at the school and college level. It takes them a step ahead of plain expression of thoughts to contradiction of opposing thoughts and ideas. They also learn to provide alternate solutions.

Since debating is a formal interactive discussion, learning to debate prepares a person to speak at clubs and organisations where a variety of opinions are offered. It is also common to have debates in democratic bodies like the local Municipal Corporations, legislative assemblies and parliaments around the world. Noted legislators and statesmen are known to be capable speakers.

Debating in schools and colleges is limited to speaking on a given subject when one member of the team speaks in favour of the subject, and the other against it. Since the subject is given in advance and each speaker

40

has a fixed timeframe to speak, the participants prepare the matter in advance. The skills are judged by the way the matter is presented, and also how the speaker deviates from the written speech to challenge what an opposing speaker has said. The lead speakers are allowed additional time to give closing remarks before putting the matter to the house for vote.

When a person is confident about personal debating skills and is knowledgeable, one can participate in extempore debates where the subject is announced shortly before the contest. This gives a limited time to prepare. A person relies upon personal knowledge of the subject, the ability to place the thoughts in correct order, and use effective speaking skills. This is not easy. However, this is the real test of the person's knowledge and speaking skills. One develops confidence by being well informed and through practice whenever an occasion presents itself. Eventually one emerges as a good speaker.

Schools and colleges provide debating opportunities also through organisation of simulated legislatures such as the Model United Nations, where students represent different countries, or a Mock Parliament, where students represent different political parties and express their opinions on a subject that is relevant on the occasion. Another variation is a moot court and a mock trial for students studying law and similar subjects.

Extempore debating provides a good foundation for young people to participate in group discussions, which form a part of the admission process for many college courses after school. These also provide opportunities to develop the confidence and skills for situations that require negotiating in everyday life. The discussion during study of case histories in a variety of situations also requires the ability to think logically swiftly, and use good speaking skills. Each effort leads to the next, helping to gradually build confidence and skills to face the needs of a successful life.

EMOTIONAL APPEAL

Another important element that all outstanding public speakers use is to touch the audience emotionally with whatever they speak. Even in everyday dialogue, individuals who can touch the feelings and emotions in others draw immediate attention. The audience reacts immediately because the message convinces them that the speaker knows how they feel. They can identify their own thoughts with what is being said. They appreciate the superiority of the speaker in being able to read their thoughts.

In everyday life we see how people are attracted to songs and music that touches them emotionally. It gives them a feeling of inner satisfaction. It is observed that patriotic poems, prayers and songs exert a motivating influence. Devotional songs and music have a soothing influence. They attract a person to a higher form of life. Religious leaders all over the world are known to touch the feelings and emotions of the audience when they quote from religious texts. They convey a message that God loves everyone.

It is not easy for all speakers to touch the audience emotionally. Only speakers with a positive personality and confidence can do this. Only virtuous persons who are endowed with great inner strength can move people emotionally. To be effective in this direction it would be necessary for a person to develop personal magnetism.

Personal virtues lend strength to the speaker. One is then able to touch others. Of all virtues, love and benevolence are the greatest. One who can love unconditionally can influence everyone.

PREPARATION

Public speaking skills begin with confidence and a desire to communicate one's ideas to others. To achieve this aim it is necessary that the person must have a good knowledge, listening skills, reading skills and the ability to speak clearly in a language that the audience can understand. Taking part in declamation contests and debates help develop speaking skills. Before one is ready to speak, the person must prepare the details point-by-point of the message that is to be communicated to the audience.

All good speakers agree that it takes almost ten times the time to prepare for a formal presentation. For example, if one were to prepare a half-hour speech, it would take almost five hours to research and collect data, write it well in order of priority and practise before making the presentation. When a person takes preparation for granted, the presentation cannot be expected to be effective. The preparation is an essential element of an effective speech.

Think it over...

Sincerity is to speak as we think, to do as we pretend and profess, to perform what we promise, and really to be what we would seem and appear to be.

— *Tillotson*

PUBLIC SPEAKING

History has witnessed the use of this ability for both good and evil. While everyone is aware of gurus and leaders, who are known to have motivated people to good and productive acts, we cannot ignore the evil perpetrated by dictators. Many of them were very persuasive speakers. They presented negative thoughts as attractive and useful and wrecked havoc in the lives of millions of people.

Public speaking skills can be traced to the times when mankind began to use speech as a medium of communication. At one time oratory was known to have developed into a fine art. With time, public speaking skills have changed towards greater practical usage not only by leaders and politicians, but also by common people in everyday life. Many young people are attracted to develop this ability, and seek knowledge by joining institutions that provide training in speaking skills. Several institutions of national and international repute provide training.

Public speaking is a fine art. Many people try to learn it. Only a few achieve recognition. Skilled public speakers confirm that they learnt the art through keen observation, preparation and the art of effective delivery. A good knowledge of the basics is essential. Ultimately it is the choice of correct words, control over the voice, innovative presentation, and the use of gestures that makes it effective.

Good speakers can gauge audience reaction quickly. They use a variety of methods to draw attention and touch the emotional chord in the mind of the listeners. It is common to use humour to bridge the gap between the speaker and the audience. However, only capable speakers can do it effectively. Speakers who can hold attention of the audience soon develop a relationship that ensures an effective transfer of information and ideas.

An important element of public speaking is that a good speaker knows when the message has been effectively conveyed, and stops speaking, leaving the audience thirsting for just 'a little more'.

A good public speaker is never just a good speaker only. In his or her own right, a good public speaker is a leader. This is natural because speaking skills come only from a high level of knowledge in one or more fields. The knowledge and experience form the foundation. Good speaking skills make the communication effective. The purpose of the speech is achieved.

POINTS TO PONDER

1. Gaining self-confidence is the first step to becoming a good speaker.

2. A magnetic personality helps to gain the confidence of the audience.

3. It is not possible to speak convincingly without the knowledge of the language.

4. Positive body language helps to make a presentation effective.

5. One must learn to differentiate between information, knowledge and wisdom.

6. One must first be a good listener before becoming a good speaker.

7. The quality of the voice is important for effective speaking.

8. Correct phonetics help make a speech clear and effective.

9. Reading is essential to update one's knowledge.

10. One begins to learn public speaking through elocution contests and debates in schools and colleges.

11. A speech with an emotional appeal is always effective.

12. A speech becomes effective with good preparation.

13. Good speaking skills lead a person to leadership roles.

Developing Speaking Skills

After a person is aware of various elements that together contribute to the skills and abilities of a good public speaker, the next step is to know how these skills and abilities can be acquired or learned.

It is essential to understand that no public speaker was born with speaking skills and abilities. Like other skills these have to be learnt. One needs to know what is required, and where the information is available. It is also necessary to understand the direction in which the effort has to be made.

Each person is different. The life of each person is ruled by personal strengths and weaknesses. Since these vary from one person to another, the methods used to acquire speaking skills and abilities will also need to be different, to be in harmony with the individual's personality. Every person will need to assess personal requirements, and adopt methods to move towards the goal.

What are your goals? The major goal would obviously be to become a good public speaker. What is holding you back from attaining your goal? Do you have the necessary confidence to speak in public? If not, then what is holding you back? Is it the fear of standing before a group that frightens you? Or do you blank out when you stand up to speak? It could also be that lack of knowledge of your own subject robs you of your confidence? Or is it that you are unable to create the necessary rapport with the audience?

In the last step we learned about the elements that contribute to help an individual to become a good public speaker. Let us study step by step how you can get over your own limitations one by one, and acquire the necessary skills.

Think it over...

Confidence imparts a wondrous inspiration to its possessor. It bears him on in security, either to meet no danger, or to find matter of glorious trial.

— *Milton*

BUILDING SPEAKING CONFIDENCE

A variety of fears haunt most people. These fears restrict their growth and potential. Of all the fears, the fear of speaking before a group of people is rated the highest, next only to the fear of death.

The fear, combined with apprehension and worry, leads to anxiety. This is visible, as the skin turns pale, accompanied by sweating, nausea, chill and trembling. Anxiety has several components. The expectation of a sudden uncertain danger is known to trigger the reaction. When asked to speak in public, the danger is that of not knowing what to speak, or forgetting what one desires to speak and of being ridiculed and made the laughing stock before a group of people.

As soon as the danger is perceived, the body reacts immediately to deal with the emergency. The mouth feels dry, the blood pressure rises, and the pulse beats faster. There is sweating to cope with the situation. The digestive system is also affected. The most common reaction is nausea. Many need to run to the toilet. The person feels shortness of breath. There is a feeling of chill and trembling. The skin turns pale. The immediate reaction is to avoid and run away from the source of anxiety.

Some confuse the symptoms to be pathological. In reality, the cause is lack of adaptability to a particular situation. If the person were mentally prepared to face the situation, there would be no fear, anxiety, or any of the symptoms just discussed.

The situation is also known as stage fright, speech anxiety, performance anxiety, speech phobia and shyness. Similar symptoms affect stage performers, singers and speakers. The symptoms may appear long before the actual performance. They become visible as soon as the fear of the performance is anticipated. Many believe that only people who are not prepared or are newcomers experience these problems. Even the most experienced persons are known to experience this anxiety. However, they have learned not to let the anxiety go out of hand and become a nuisance.

A large number of people turn to doctors for help. Initially, the family doctor may prescribe one of the many anti-anxiety drugs that are available today. Some of the patients are referred to psychiatrists for long-term treatment. The doctors treat the condition as a pathological manifestation because the patients are unable to explain that the symptoms are triggered by an imaginary fear of speaking or performing before a group of people.

With relief coming from the drugs prescribed by the family doctor or the psychiatrist, many people begin to use these drugs regularly. Diazepam is one of them. Beta-blockers are also used to treat some forms of anxiety. Users fail to realise that many of these drugs are habit-forming and addictive. They make one feel good, and also confident, though temporarily. Over a period, many side effects may emerge, giving rise to several new problems.

Since the problem emerges from a fear, glossophobia, the fear of speaking in public, the treatment should aim at teaching the person to cope with the imaginary situation, and thus control the cause of the problem. Since this method requires psychological adjustment and effort, many prefer the use of drugs, tobacco and even alcohol. Those who are aware of the dangers of drugs turn to alternative remedies like homeopathic medication, or even use of plant extracts like Valerian root, passionflower, hops, chamomile and Hypericum perforatum.

How does one learn to cope with the situation without depending upon some of the crutches people use? The answer lies in controlling your mind. This, in turn, means controlling your thoughts.

Does it mean that one should ignore the situation because it is imaginary? No. Ignoring a situation means that you are accepting it, but trying to avoid it. That is no solution. You need to face the situation. It is a fear. Like any other fear, you need to face it to overcome it. How do people suffering from the fear of darkness control it? By acting brave and going into the darkness to appreciate that there is nothing to fear. What do people do when they are afraid what would happen to their family if they were to die? They buy life insurance to protect their families in the event of untimely death. Do things that counter the fear.

How does one get over the fear of speaking in public? The ideal way is to develop the confidence to face the public and speak to them. This confidence cannot be developed overnight. The foundation of confidence lies in the individual's mind. One must believe in personal ability. One must be able to appreciate the advantage of being able to speak. When the person thinks of the many benefits that will accrue to him or her with the ability to speak in public, the person is motivated to make the effort to gain self-confidence, which is the key to getting over the fear of speaking.

Self-confidence comes from belief in one's ability to deliver, to succeed. One must visualise personal success. The greater and deeper the visualisation, the motivation to succeed that emerges will be stronger. Do not aim at big successes in the beginning. Look for smaller successes. Each small success prepares a person for a little bigger success the next time. This way, one day, even the bigger successes will look commonplace.

The smallest of successes is not possible without preparation. Therefore, when you visualise success, also visualise yourself preparing for that success. Put in your very best efforts. Your success depends upon it. Do not be easily satisfied with your efforts. With each effort, improve upon your performance. Practice. Put in as much practice as you can. The more you do it, the better it will sink into your subconscious. It will help you in time of need.

Be well prepared in every way. When you are prepared for a situation, you know what is coming, and will be able to face it calmly. Do not place any trust upon drugs or alcohol. These can only ruin your performance. Their use can bring in newer problems. To avoid digestive problems eat less. Be in the company of confident people. Talk of things of common interest. Laugh. Laughter helps control nervousness.

Arrive a little earlier than you are expected to. Acquaint yourself with the surroundings, the place where you will be seated, the lectern, the placing of the mike and the public address system. Talk to people. That will keep your mind away from your own thoughts. If you can, just close your eyes and look within to talk to God within you. One of the most outstanding attributes of God is patience. When we seek blessings from God, visualise the blessings coming in the form of His patience. Breathe deeply to feel the patience. Visualise public appreciation. Visualise success.

When you are invited to speak, walk confidently to the lectern. Stand confidently, taking a few deep breaths, look around at the audience with a smile. Build eye contact with the audience, as you begin your speech. You have been invited to give of your best. That is exactly what you will do. Your efforts on the preparation will be amply rewarded when your speech is well received. Do remember that the audience is constituted of people with different mindsets. It is never possible to please everyone. But you can feel the appreciation when the audience applauds. Use this success as the stepping-stone to the next success that awaits you. With each success, your self-confidence will grow from within, taking you towards your goal.

Think it over...

The greatest results in life are usually attained by simple means and the exercise of ordinary qualities. These may for the most part be summed in these two – common sense and perseverance.

— *Feltham*

MAKE SUCCESS A COMPANION

When self-confidence emerges from success and, in turn, success comes from confidence and preparation, a person must make success a constant companion. This will reflect not only in public speaking, but also in other areas of life.

Like everything else in life, success also begins with a thought. Through this thought a person visualises a dream, a dream to be a capable person, to be able to achieve great things. From the dream emerges a desire – a desire to turn the dream into tangible reality. Desires motivate people to act.

Think success. Visualise yourself as successful. Visualise yourself of possessing good speaking skills. Remind yourself that you will make the effort to turn your dreams into reality. Prepare a *Plan of Action*. Set goals pertaining to acquiring speaking skills. Set deadlines. Act. Work towards success.

Seek the friendship and support of good people. Seek the help of people who are knowledgeable, people who can guide and help you in your efforts. In turn, appreciate them. Be grateful for their support. At all times avoid people who discourage you. Avoid them even if they do it only to caution you against pitfalls. Do not let small setbacks upset you. Do not panic. The world won't come to an end. Obstacles are a part of life. Problems come and go.

To attain success volunteer to speak on special occasions, even if only to introduce or thank a speaker. The exercise will provide useful practice, and will also gradually build a chain of successes for you. Observe etiquette and manners. Communicate well through positive body language. You will soon be known for your speaking skills.

POSITIVE BODY LANGUAGE

Positive body language is an important element of effective public speaking. Many argue that when body language is involuntary, how can we control it? Is it not something that just happens? What can we do about it?

The body language immediately communicates the level of confidence of the speaker. It also reflects the level of preparedness. The audience judges a speaker in line with their perception. It is really the speaker who knows best about levels of self-confidence and preparedness.

The situation is like that of a student who is asked by the teacher if he has done his homework. If he has, he will be confident. The teacher reads the confidence from the expression on the face, from the way he responds. If he has not done the homework, he has two choices. The first is to tell the truth. The second is to tell a lie that he has done it. What does the student do to cover up the lie? He speaks with pretence of confidence. If he does not, the body language will let out the truth. The teacher would then like to see it. To cover up he will need to tell another lie that he has left the work at home.

Like the student, the speaker needs to project an image of confidence. Even if he does not feel as confident as he would like to be, still it is important that the speaker must pretend to be confident. This is often described as showmanship. You can see it in the person who serves as the Master of Ceremonies at a function. You can see it in the anchors on television shows. People want to hear a person who has something to say with confidence. If the speaker is not confident about what to say, why should the audience waste their time on hearing what is not important?

Positive body language demands that the speaker must appear responsible. He must arrive on time. He must be appropriately dressed. The expression on the face must be one of confidence and friendship. The etiquette and good manners must be visible from the behaviour, the smile and the way he greets and meets people. Even as he sits waiting for his turn to speak, the image must be one of confidence. All the eyes are on the speaker.

To project positive body language, the speaker must be well prepared to make a great speech. Confidence comes from the advance preparation. At the same time, the speaker must possess qualities of showmanship, of being more capable than the others. This requires that the communication skills must be well developed to meet a variety of situations.

Think it over…

Language is not only the vehicle of thought; it is a great and efficient instrument in thinking.

— *Sir H. Davy*

KNOWLEDGE OF THE LANGUAGE

A speaker needs to be well versed with the language that is used to convey ideas and information to the audience. The language is a medium and a communication is not possible without it. However, the knowledge of the speaker and the audience is not always balanced. The knowledge of the speaker should be superior. At the same time it is necessary that the speaker must speak at a level that the audience can understand.

All languages initially emerged as spoken languages. A spoken language is the use of words spoken to convey a message to another person. When many people use the same words to convey similar meanings, a spoken language develops gradually. The written languages followed later when it became necessary to record what is verbally said. These develop slowly. In contrast to the spoken language, the written language is refined and follows a definite system. It can be observed that the spoken languages vary from one region to another, with changed accents and dialects, sometimes making it difficult for people from different regions to understand each other.

English is an international language, used freely to develop trade and industry around the world. Even within United Kingdom, the home of Queen's English, the accents and dialects of the spoken language are different. The written language is common. The English spoken in U.S.A., Canada, Australia and several other countries sounds different from the English spoken in U.K.

A language is a living entity. It is undergoing a change all the time. According to need, people 'invent' new sounds and words, or even adapt them from other languages. For example, 'guru' is a Hindi word meaning a preceptor, mentor or a spiritual teacher. However, it has now been adapted into written English, meaning an influential teacher or expert, as we see it commonly used: for example, a management guru. Many such words are being adapted into English and other languages.

The spoken language is the real language, or the mother tongue. One learns it from the parents and the family. It is the authentic language, and has its own grammar and style. The written language is adapted from the spoken language. It is always a refined, or revised version. Even within the same language, the written language has variations in spellings and forms of words, as we observe in the English used in England and U.S.A. For example, 'centre' is spelt 'center', or 'realise' is spelt 'realize'. This has much to do with the spoken language, and its usage by a large number of people.

The speaker's principal medium to convey ideas and information is through the spoken language. It is not possible without a good knowledge of the language. Even with the knowledge of the language, the speaker must have the ability to choose words that convey the message effectively. The choice of the words is not easy. All speakers and writers would confirm it. While writing, it is easier to choose words. There are no compulsions of time to put it on paper. While speaking, the choice of words has to be spontaneous. This can be difficult unless the person has a good vocabulary of the particular language. While speaking, the words must flow. The listener can get impatient if there are gaps in the speech. With the listener getting irritated the speech may fail completely. All public speakers have faced such situations. To be effective, one must be armed with the appropriate words. Leave the rest to the audience.

THE ENGLISH LANGUAGE

English is a colourful language. It has an estimated 500,000 words, expressing varying shades of meaning. Some insist that the number of words is higher.

How large is your vocabulary? Some people have a vocabulary of a few thousand words. Most people go through life with a vocabulary of only a few hundred words.

Every person has two kinds of vocabulary — receptive vocabulary and an active vocabulary. The receptive vocabulary includes words, which you can understand when you hear or read them. The active vocabulary includes words, which you use to express yourself through the spoken and written language. There is always a big gap between the two. To be effective, the aspiring public speaker needs to strengthen the vocabulary and improve upon the power of expression. The gap between the receptive and the active vocabulary must be reduced. Words that are understood must be brought into active use when speaking and writing.

The study of words is an interesting exercise. One discovers new words and meanings. All good speakers and writers make the dictionary their constant companion. Whenever in doubt one must check the meaning of the word, which is not clear. Try to learn and use new words everyday. If one were to learn one new word everyday, at the end of the year one would know 365 additional words. Note new words and the meaning in a notebook. Review them periodically. Get yourself a thesaurus and a book of synonyms and antonyms. You will be surprised at the range of words that have similar meanings, and yet the shade of meaning varies for each word. One would also do well to buy a book on increasing 'word-power'. Words are important tools for a public speaker.

To improve your language skills give special attention to:

- Improving your vocabulary
- Using correct pronunciation
- Drafting grammatically correct sentences
- Not using hackneyed phrases.

ORGANISE THE SPEECH

Even the best speakers do not make a spontaneous speech. They only *appear* to be doing so effortlessly. In reality, they have already put in a lot of effort before the speech is made. The speech is best prepared in the comfort of one's home. It must be written just as the speaker would like to present it.

Before the speaker begins to write the speech, the purpose must be clearly understood. If the purpose is not clear, forget about it altogether. No speech has ever been effective without a purpose. The speech must be written with the purpose uppermost in the mind.

Most people become self-conscious and blank out when they sit to write. This fear is somewhat like stage fright all speakers are well acquainted with. Relax! Take a rough paper. Imagine that the audience you wish to talk to is sitting across the table. Unfortunately, the audience cannot hear. Therefore, you need to communicate your message to them in writing. Write, as you would speak.

What is the message? Write down each point that you would like to make — just as though you were speaking. Have you got all the points right? Now mark them in order of preference by placing 1, 2, and 3 and so on against each. When you finally present the points to the audience, you would want to arrange them according to their importance. Once you have the priorities sorted out, you can prepare the final written speech.

When speaking, the first challenge is to draw the attention of the audience. The opening sentences of the speech must draw immediate attention. They must arouse the interest of the audience, who must want to know more about the subject. Speakers use a variety of techniques to make this possible.

In the main body of the presentation divide each idea or point into a paragraph. Proceed logically. Common points can be put together in a paragraph. Write short paragraphs. They make the presentation easier. Use simple words. Write short sentences. They make crisp listening and are easy to understand. As you write, ask yourself: Is my message clear? Is it concise? Is it convincing? Is it complete? When you answer 'yes' to these questions, you have done your best.

Your 'best' need not necessarily be the last word on the subject. Let us not forget: there is always a better way of doing the same thing. If it were not so, all progress would come to a stand still. Therefore, make it a habit to revise what you have written. Ask yourself: can I improve upon it? If you can, go ahead and do it. Let the work bear the stamp of perfection.

All this sounds simple. But it is not so. One learns it only through practice. It involves knowledge of the language and good writing skills. The person must have the ability to think in terms of how others will interpret the words and expressions used. The more one writes the sooner one learns the techniques that work. Observe the work of others. Look for the best. Adapt ideas to suit your style. Soon you will be writing excellent speeches.

The closing of the presentation should be like the knockout punch of the boxer. The message should hit the audience hard. It should get them to think and act. This will require thoughtful preparation that comes slowly with experience.

When preparing the speech follow these simple rules:

- Begin with an attractive opening.
- Use a language that the audience can easily understand. Academicians may appreciate pedantic language, not the common person.
- Use words that are easily understood. When choosing between two words, select one that is easier to understand. For example, book, tome, volume and publication have similar meanings, but 'book' is the easiest to understand.

- Stick to the point. Most people have a tendency to deviate from the subject.
- The subject must progress logically, just as B follows A, and C follows B.
- Write as few words as possible. After you have written, revise the text to condense it by keeping the essentials, and trimming the frills.
- Do not repeat what the audience already knows. They will lose interest.
- Avoid clichés and unnecessary phrases.
- Use simple words. For example, "in the event of" could be replaced with "if".
- Adopt a positive outlook. Always avoid the negative.
- When you have written what you feel conveys your message, just stop.
- Have a closing punch line, which compels the audience to act.
- Keep revising the presentation until you are satisfied.

Think it over...

A printed speech is like a dried flower: the substance, indeed, is there, but the colour is faded and the perfume gone.

— *Lorain*

HOW DOES THE PRESENTATION SOUND?

After you have completed writing the speech, and also revised it, read it loudly as though you were addressing the audience. How does it sound? Does it convey the message you need to present? Will it fulfil the purpose you have in mind? Do you see any ambiguities that could be misinterpreted? You still have the time to polish it. If it needs to be polished, do it now.

Time yourself. Will your speech fit into the timeframe allotted to you? If you exceed the time allotted to you, you will need to trim the presentation to fit into the timeframe. Many speakers exert their importance by taking the liberty of exceeding the time given to them. This is not right. This might pamper the speaker's vanity, but the audience does not appreciate it. It has been observed that the audience compares the time allotted in the programme, and the actual time taken by the speaker. Every little thing contributes to the opinion of the audience.

MAKING NOTES

The purpose of writing the speech is not to read it word by word. In some cases where a lot of technical information is to be presented, as observed in technical seminars, the presentation is read, with copies distributed amongst the participating delegates, who may be technically as qualified as the speaker. This gives the audience an opportunity to think, debate and add on to knowledge on the subject. However, it has been observed that when reading a speech, it is not possible for the speaker to make eye contact or create rapport with the audience. This makes it a little impersonal, robbing it of spontaneity.

To avoid this limitation of reading, most speakers do not read the speech directly. They read it several times at home to almost memorise the sequence of the points and also the key words that help achieve the purpose. As additional support, the speaker transfers the key ideas on to blank cards — 3 inches by 5 inches. Each point is numbered and written boldly on the card. This helps in maintaining continuity. Cards are easy to carry. The speaker places them on the lectern and glances at them to confirm that the written speech is delivered in logical order. This makes it necessary that the notes on the cards must be carefully made with the original written speech as the basic material.

TOUCHING THE AUDIENCE EMOTIONALLY

Speakers who know what the audience likes and wants to hear are always effective in conveying their message. All outstanding speakers are known to touch the audience emotionally whenever they speak. Even in everyday conversations individuals who appreciate the feelings and emotions in others are always respected. The speaker and the audience get connected because of mutual respect. They perceive the similarity of thoughts. The speaker speaks from a superior position.

Words alone are not enough to touch people emotionally. The positive personality of the speaker has a message of its own. The positive outlook towards life helps words to emerge from within. The words are spoken with utter sincerity backed by conviction and confidence. Only people with character and integrity possess the ability to move the audience emotionally. These qualities are rare and built upon a virtuous life. The virtues in the speaker help the audience in accepting him or her as a dependable person and the message as useful. Truth, honesty and thoughtfulness of others stand out in the speaker. Those who love unconditionally easily influence everyone.

Think it over...

The passions are the only orators that always succeed. They are, as it were, nature's art of eloquence, fraught with infallible rules. Simplicity, with the aid of the passions, persuades more than the utmost eloquence without it.

— *Rochefoucauld*

UNDERSTANDING HUMAN NATURE

Since times immemorial there has been a continuous effort to promote understanding in mankind. Human nature is such that even when success is attained in this field, there will be some opposed to it. Soon they bring the effort to naught. This has gone on with mankind making and unmaking its own destiny. God has endowed every person the right to choose whatever way he or she wishes to think, act or live. Constraints, if any, are man-made.

An understanding of human nature is essential for a public speaker to be effective. As a speaker, it is not possible to touch people emotionally unless you can understand them. The aspiring public speakers wonder how is it possible to understand human nature when elderly people confess that with all their experience they are still learning about it.

The public speaker can leave the study of the psyche and the mindset of people to the psychologists who specialise in the field. It should suffice to understand that three basic instincts or desires drive everyone. If one can understand how these influence a person it becomes easy to understand human sensitivity. The knowledge can be used to touch the feelings and emotions of the audience.

Self-preservation is the first concern of every person. Everyone wants to live. Every person is sensitive about everything pertaining to life. This includes good nutrition, health and well-being. It also includes a vocation and everything else connected with it. Whenever anything endangers a person's life, it touches the innermost self and arouses an alarm.

Reproduction of one's kind is the second concern of every person. Everyone wants to become immortal through one's children. This is possible through a family, wife, children and a home. Everyone is very sensitive about everything pertaining to these. It has been observed that anything that endangers these relationships immediately arouses an alarm and sets a person to action.

Power over others is the third concern of every person. Everyone seeks self-esteem. Beyond it, when a person has a vocation and a family, a person seeks to develop power over other people. People use different methods to achieve this. In ancient times, physical strength was the source of power. Now it is manifested in other forms.

In the present times, people achieve success in this field by amassing great fortunes. We know that money is power. People live in houses larger than their needs. They own cars and luxuries. They hold membership in clubs and other organisations. They aspire for high positions and offices to command power. Whenever anything connected to 'power' is endangered, the person reacts immediately.

The public speaker will do well to understand that the audience is receptive to anything that helps it pamper anyone of the three basic driving forces. For example, who would not like to hear a speaker explain how to live a 100 years? Who would not like to hear how to have a loving family? Or, who would not want to know how to make a fortune in the next five years of your life? Equally so, the audience would love to hear a speaker tell them how to become a leader in their community? Observe the titles of the books in any bookshop. Every book aims to help people fulfil their basic desires. In the same way, a good public speaker learns to touch the sensitivities of the audience, and once this is done it becomes easy to convey the message of the speech.

PRESENTATION AND PHONETICS

On any occasion it is the way a subject is presented to the audience that decides the ultimate effect. Over a period, every public speaker develops a style that is identified with him or her. Even when two speakers speak on the same subject and convey similar points of view, the effect of the two speeches will never be the same. This can be attributed to the speaker's style of presentation.

It is this style, which differentiates one speaker from the other. The speaking style does not develop overnight. It comes gradually, as one speaks on a variety of subjects over a period. The style reflects the way a person wants to put across ideas and information. Since each person thinks differently, the style of speaking will also be different.

How can "style" in speaking be defined? It is easier to observe and appreciate it rather than define it in words.

When speaking, the words do not only convey the message, but together they also create a rhythmic effect, which can be pleasing, and sometimes not so. The words reflect the thoughts, the ideology and the attitude of the speaker. The style reflects the personality.

When learning to speak, a person must appreciate that a style is something personal. It develops only when a person is truly the personal self, and not somebody else. To be able to do so, one must resolve to be natural and comfortable with what one is, and not copy someone else.

Most people are guilty of copying others. If one were to observe people and adapt ideas how they succeed and live better, it would be appreciated. However, when one copies style blindly, as in clothes, mannerisms and speaking, it does not take long to observe and feel the lack of originality. To be original and convincing, the simple secret is: "be yourself!"

An important aspect of speaking in public is the speaker's ability to speak loud and clear. Unless each word is correctly pronounced it can be easily misinterpreted. This requires the speaker to have a good pronunciation and the ability to speak keeping the punctuation marks in mind. Phonetics is concerned with the study of different aspects of human speech. Every aspiring public speaker must be acquainted with it.

A speaker will do well to speak to an audience just as one were to speak in everyday life — in plain simple words, directed at the person you are talking to. If you can speak convincingly to one person, you should be able to speak equally convincingly to a group of people. The personal style of speaking will develop over a period of time, as you make an effort to speak in conformity with the techniques already discussed.

POINTS TO PONDER

1. Conquering the fear of speaking in public begins from gaining self-confidence.

2. Self-confidence comes from small successes in everyday life. Make success your companion.

3. Project positive body language at all times.

4. The speaker must speak a language that is understood by the audience.

5. A speech must first be well written in complete detail.

6. Test your speech at home before presenting it to the audience.

7. Notes help make a good presentation.

8. The speaker must understand human nature before he or she can touch them emotionally.

9. Phonetics and presentation techniques are important to an effective speaker.

Making the Speech Effective

Irrespective of the fact whether a speech is for 5 minutes, or for 30 minutes, what matters ultimately is how effective is the presentation. Many factors together contribute to the effectiveness of a speech.

Every organiser desires that the purpose of the meeting being organised is achieved. To enable this, the organiser looks for and invites persons to speak on subjects that would fulfil the purpose of the meeting. The meeting is organised at a venue that is convenient to the participants. Invitations are sent out in time. To make it attractive for the audience the highlights of the programme are given special emphasis. In general, the meeting is promoted to ensure the participation of the designated delegates for whom the meeting has been organised.

Once the venue is selected, appropriate arrangements made, and the presence of the participants ensured, the success finally rests upon the speeches made by the speakers. The effectiveness of the speech depends upon several important factors. The speaker must be careful about each aspect. Let us try to understand them one by one.

UNDERSTAND THE AUDIENCE

Before a person can undertake a speaking assignment it is essential that he or she must know the purpose of the meeting and the kind of people who will form the audience. If this is not done, the speaker can be in for a rude shock. If the audience does not understand what the speaker has to say, or is capable of saying, it does not matter how knowledgeable the speaker may be, the presentation will fall flat.

It is common to invite professors and lecturers from colleges and universities to speak to students in schools, or to address groups involved in social welfare activities, people who are not fully versed with technicalities of the subject. Under such circumstances, if the speaker were to use the language and terms used in the university, the audience would not understand anything. The presentation would not be well taken.

When a professor incharge of public relations in a university speaks to underprivileged children studying in middle school about the scholarships available for underprivileged young people studying in his university, can the speech have any effect on the young minds? The children are still struggling in school. It would be a few years before they pass out and can think of going to college. How can we be sure what the situation would be like then?

In the same way, if a senior engineer were to address a group of villagers on the new technology used in making a bridge that would enable them to go to town round the year, would it help? The villagers would not be interested in hearing about the technology used, but rather the benefits that will accrue to them because of the bridge.

Laymen want to hear what benefits them, and that too in a language that they can understand.

Even when the speaker is clear about the type of audience he or she is going to speak to, and prepares an appropriate speech, it may still become necessary to make amends at the last moment. There may be too many speakers lined up. The audience may already be fed up hearing and may become restive. Under such circumstances the audience cannot be expected to be responsive. The speech would fall on unwilling ears. Only an experienced speaker can steer through such a situation.

Sometimes the audience may flare up because of some misunderstanding or lapse on the part of the organisers. An experienced speaker can immediately notice that the audience is "switched off". They are sitting in the hall, but their minds are elsewhere. This situation again requires very delicate handling. Good experienced speakers are known to "turn them on", but it is not easy. A good sense of humour helps, but it is tact and patience that are important.

The audience is invariably formed of many individuals, and each time the circumstances and the situations may be different. The speaker will need to gauge the situation and act accordingly. Success comes with experience.

Think it over...

You may deceive all the people part of the time, and part of the people all the time, but not all the people all the time.

— *Lincoln*

THE PURPOSE OF THE PRESENTATION

Next to knowing the audience, it is important for the speaker to know the purpose of the presentation. The speaker must appreciate that a speech can enlighten, entertain or motivate the audience. Entertaining is a specialised line and concerns the show business rather than the business world or the everyday life in our communities. It is informing and motivating the audience that concerns most public speakers.

The speaker must clearly understand the idea he or she wishes to sell to the audience through the speech. Unless the speaker is completely convinced of the validity of the idea, is it ever possible to sell it to the audience? Any misunderstanding on this point can make the speech ineffective.

When the management of a school informed the staff that they had invited a speaker to talk to them, the general impression was that in all likelihood the management was not happy with the performance of the staff. Perhaps this was one way to reprimand them. The speaker was experienced. He knew the purpose and could also read the mind of the audience. The teachers were surprised when the speaker said he would speak on how they could live and perform better in everyday life. He did not talk to them from the management's point of view, but from their individual points of view. The ultimate purpose of the speech was that efficient people served better. Both the organisers and the audience were happy with the outcome of the presentation. The audience was enthusiastic and confident of performing well. The purpose of the presentation was achieved because the speaker understood it well.

It is necessary that the speaker must clearly understand what is to be achieved through the speech. Once the speaker knows which way to go, preparing the speech becomes easy. With every step the speaker must bring the audience closer to the goal.

THE ALLOTTED TIME

The time allotted for a speech is important. The speakers always desire more time. The organisers are always stingy about it. Besides, it is common knowledge that it is difficult to have the audience listening to the best of speakers for a long time. A fair balance needs to be made. Many times the organisers are compelled to include several subjects on the programme. This leaves them with time constraints.

The speaker must appreciate the time constraints of the organisers and should restrict the speech to the time allotted for the purpose. The organisers do not expect the speaker to give a 30-minute presentation in 5 minutes. If only 5 to 8 minutes are allotted for a subject, the organisers expect a condensed version of the subject. The real ability of the speaker lies in condensing the speech to satisfy the organisers and the audience. Such a presentation is often likened to a bikini — it must be brief and yet should cover the essentials!

The organisers once went to a politician to invite him to speak at their function. The politician inquired for how long did they expect him to speak.

"Sir, 10 minutes have been provided in the programme," one organiser said.

The politician responded, "No, I cannot come. You said the function was due in four days. For making a 10-

minute speech I need at least a week."

The organisers wanted to compromise. Considering that there were four days to go, one of them said, "Sir, since you feel the time is short, you could speak for 5 minutes."

The politician sat up, as though shocked, "5 minutes? For a 5-minute presentation I will need at least 15 days."

The organisers had known the politician to be a vociferous speaker. One organiser inquired, "Sir, how long does it take you to prepare for a one-hour speech?"

The politician smiled, "I am ready. I can come just now."

WRITING THE SPEECH

No speaker can expect to be effective unless the speech is prepared step by step to achieve the purpose at hand. The speaker should never feel that it is just a 5-minute presentation, and therefore should take little time to prepare. That is not true. The shorter the presentation, more time it takes to prepare.

To make the speech effective, initially, do not prepare it on the basis of the time that has been allotted for the purpose. Just forget about it. Think of the purpose you need to achieve through the speech. Keeping the purpose in mind, write all that you will need to say to convince the prospective audience. Reinforce your thoughts with those of other learned people to convince the audience of the validity of the thoughts and ideas that you present. Write as well and convincingly as you possibly can.

Read the matter by yourself. Does it sound convincing? Polish the text wherever you find rough edges.

Re-read it. How does it feel now? How many minutes did it take you to read it? Will it fit into the time slot allotted to you? Probably not! You will need to edit it to bring it to the size the organisers want it to be. This is not an easy job. In the script mark all the important points that emphasize what you need to say. Keep these, and trim the rest. Re-write the shorter speech. You will now have the speech that you need to deliver.

Can short speeches be effective? Young speakers express their doubt frequently. The truth is that the shorter speeches are more effective than long speeches. Shorter speeches are well prepared. They hold the attention of the audience better. For this reason they achieve their purpose immediately.

No book on becoming an effective speaker can be complete without the mention of President Abraham Lincoln's address on the battlefield at Gettysburg. The President was not known for his oratory. Many advised him not to speak on the occasion. However, he had a purpose to achieve. There was need for peace in a warring nation where people were involved in a civil war. It is said that the President wrote the speech once, and then again and again. The people did not believe he could do it. But he had a purpose, and that guided him to limit the speech to just a few lines — lines that have become immortal for how much can be said in such a few words. Read it for yourself.

The President said: "Fourscore and seven years ago our fathers brought forth on this continent a new nation, conceived in liberty and dedicated to the proposition that all men are created equal. Now we are engaged in a great civil war, testing whether that nation, or any nation so conceived and so dedicated, can long endure. We are met on great battlefield of that war. We have come to dedicate a portion of that field as a final resting place for those who here gave their lives that that nation might live. It is altogether fitting and proper that we should do this. But, in a larger sense, we cannot dedicate — we cannot consecrate — we cannot hallow — this ground. The brave men, living and dead, who struggled here, have consecrated it far above our poor powers to add or to detract. The world will little note nor long remember what we say here, but it can never forget, what they did here. It is rather for us to be here dedicated to the great task remaining before us — that from these honoured dead we take increased devotion to that cause for which they gave the last full measure of devotion; that we here highly resolve that these dead shall not have died in vain; that this nation, under God, shall have a new birth of freedom; and that government of the people, by the people, for the people, shall not perish from the earth."

Re-read the President's speech. It says so much. It touched everyone's heart. The rest is history. There is much that we can learn by it.

Think it over...

Genuine good taste consists in saying much in few words, in choosing among our thoughts, in having order and arrangement in what we say, and in speaking with composure.

— *Fenelon*

AN ATTRACTIVE BEGINNING

A speech is made or marred with the first few sentences spoken by the speaker. Have you observed that as soon as the speaker's name is announced, everyone's attention is focussed on the speaker? The introduction of the speaker arouses further interest in the audience, who watch the way the speaker walks over to the lectern, stands there with confidence, and begins the speech.

Even before the speaker begins to speak, messages are signaled through body gestures. The audience is able to gauge the level of the speaker's confidence. This is the first step of the audience's reaction to the speaker. The next step would be when the speaker begins to speak.

It is customary for speakers to address the dignitaries on the stage and in the audience prior to the actual speech. It is often asked if it is necessary. It is not. The audience is waiting to hear the speaker, and not whom he considers worthy of mentioning in the address. The best rule is: Address the person presiding over the meeting; the chief guest, if any, and the rest could be addressed as ladies and gentlemen. That should suffice in normal usage. That would also save time and a negative reaction if an important name were missed out.

The speaker should begin the speech with an opening sentence that would immediately draw the attention of the audience. You just read a speech by President Abraham Lincoln. Observe how he started his address: "Fourscore and seven years ago our fathers brought forth on this continent a new nation, conceived in liberty and dedicated to the proposition that all men are created equal." Have you noticed how much has been conveyed in just one sentence? The audience is immediately attentive. They want to hear more.

Observe yet another great opening when President John F. Kennedy addressed the United Nations at the untimely death of Dag Hammarskjold in a plane accident in Africa: "We meet in an hour of grief and challenge. Dag Hammarskjold is deep in our hearts, but the task for which he died is at the top of our agenda. A noble servant of peace is gone, but the quest for peace lies before us."

Here is another opening by Marcus Tullius Cicero, who lived over 2,000 years ago, when he reprimanded Catiline in the meeting of the Senate: "When, O Catiline, do you mean to cease abusing our patience? How long is that madness of yours still to mock us? When is there to be an end of that unbridled audacity of yours, swaggering about as it does now?"

Some speakers begin with a touch of humour. When a person was introduced as the 'best speaker' in the organisation, the speaker responded in his opening remarks that he had conducted the survey to name the 'best speaker'. On another occasion when a speaker was lavishly introduced, in his opening remarks he said, "Thank God, my wife isn't here. She wouldn't have let the kind gentleman say all those good things about me." A few speakers begin with a joke or a story, but these must be very carefully chosen.

Besides an attractive opening the audience need to be told what is the object of the speech. The title of the speech as given in the programme will tell them what to expect. However, it is the speaker who needs to give the details. He needs to decide when and how to do it. He must state the object of the speech effectively, describe it as a problem, and do it provocatively to arouse interest.

A speaker talking to managers at the lower level said, "To day I am going to tell you how to stop working like a clerk and start working like a manager."

At a meeting of a reputed service organisation a speaker began his speech by saying, "I want to talk to you about problems that money cannot solve, problems that need to be tackled with sincere effort, courage and spirit."

The speaker should present the object of the speech so that the audience can identify itself with the problem. When they become interested, a rapport is established between the speaker and the audience.

The extra time the speaker spends in preparing an appropriate opening is well worth the while. Once the attention of the audience has been drawn and eye contact and rapport established between the speaker and the audience, it is time to elaborate the idea being sold to the audience.

THE BODY OF THE SPEECH

The body of the speech must begin with the purpose of the message, followed by the details. For example, the purpose of the speech is to seek the cooperation of the people that they must be involved with the health care facilities being provided by the government. After a good opening to draw attention, the next step would be to tell the audience how the government is trying to make the facilities available to the public, and also how these facilities function.

The next thing the audience would obviously like to know is what is lacking in the present provisions, and how they affect the people who avail of the services. It would be appropriate to give examples of how the services fell short in some cases. This reinforces what the speaker has stated.

To progress logically, the speaker should next suggest how the situation can be corrected, how better services can reach the public. Again, it would be useful if the speaker could reinforce his suggestions with examples in other places where the suggestions brought a marked change in benefits to the patients availing of the services. The audience likes to hear of what would benefit them as individuals. Health is part of the 'self-preservation need' of human beings as discussed earlier. To be effective, the speaker must place greater emphasis on the benefits rather than on the idea.

When the audience is convinced of the benefits, it is time to tell them how these benefits can be attained. The audience would like to know how they could help, what would be their role and involvement. The audience would also like to be reassured that their efforts would not be more than the benefits that will accrue, and also that their present routine will not be disturbed.

Public speaking aims at persuading the audience to accept a new idea, and put it to practice. It is an exercise in persuasion. This is not easy. To succeed, the speaker needs to be able to read the mind of the audience. He needs to understand their mental makeup. He must know what moves the audience. Only when the speaker possesses these abilities can he or she motivate others. These are essentially qualities that good leaders possess.

It would not be wrong to say that a good speaker must necessarily be a leader.

When preparing the body of the speech keep the following in mind:

- Restrict yourself to 3 or 4 major points that can be remembered easily. Do not try to cover too much ground. Avoid vague issues.

- Never tell the audience the number of points you will place before them. They begin to concentrate on the number rather than on the content.

- For each major point have sub-topics, emphatic words, phrases and sentences. Include stories to highlight a point.

- Work on each point according to priority. This makes the speech flexible. If a change is necessary in an emergency, the speech can be restricted to items of top priority.

- Working point-wise makes it easier for the speaker to deliver a speech, and for the audience to remember it.

When the speaker finds that he has precisely defined the idea, explained how it will benefit the audience, and also what needs to be done, it is time to close the presentation. It is now time for the audience to act.

Think it over...

There is no iron curtain that the aggregate sentiments of mankind cannot penetrate.

— *James F. Byrnes*

AN APT CLOSING

Most speakers tend to lose hold of the situation when they come to the close of the speech. The speaker knows that whatever was to be explained has been said. However, he may not be sure whether the audience is convinced with what has been said. To reinforce the message the speakers tend to repeat whatever has already been said. The audience does not usually take the repetition kindly, may consider it a waste of their time and may "switch off" a little prematurely, bringing the otherwise good speech to naught. The ideal thing for the speaker to do when he has said whatever he wanted to is to "shut up", thank the audience and sit down. The audience will appreciate it.

Experienced speakers do not close the speech abruptly, but gradually build it up to the point where they tell the audience how they can act. It is like throwing the ball into their court. It is now time for the audience to act. The speaker has said what he or she wanted to. It is time for the audience to think and act.

Just as it is necessary to have an attractive opening to gain the attention of the audience, it is equally important to have a challenging closing of the speech to motivate the audience to action. This requires some ingenuity and thought. An effective speaker must always plan to have an appropriate close.

Read how Swami Vivekanand summed up his address on Unity of Religions to the Parliament of Religions in Chicago: "If the Parliament of Religions has shown anything to the world it is this; it has proved to the world that holiness, purity and charity are not the exclusive possessions of any one church in the world, and that every system has produced men and women of the most exalted character. In the face of this evidence, if anybody dreams of the exclusive survival of his own religion and the destruction of others, I pity him from the bottom of my heart, and point out to him that upon the banner of every religion will soon be written, in spite of resistance: "Help and not Fight". "Assimilation and not Destruction." "Harmony and Peace and not Dissension."

The closing should be in harmony with the purpose of the presentation. It should take the audience towards the goal. The closing by Swami Vivekanand amply sums up how everyone should look at different religions.

Other speakers may want to do it with a concluding statement. For example, the Managing Director of a company may close the presentation this way: "Gentlemen, I have just informed you of the activities of the company this past year. It is now for you to decide which way you would like to take the company in the next five years. Thank you."

In the same way, a speaker talking about his love for nature and adventure tourism may close by saying: "I have learnt much from my love for the hills and mountains, the forests and the rivers. It is now your turn to experience the glory of nature. It is as easy as joining this one week's tour."

The concluding remarks will depend upon the purpose of the speech. It can end on an optimistic note, or just a plain suggestion for the audience to think about. It can also end with a request, a promise or a warning. Some end it dramatically or with a story, others with a challenge to act. Appropriate closing remarks compel the audience to think and act.

DELIVERING THE SPEECH

Even with the most disarming opening remarks, a purposeful message and challenging closing remarks, the effectiveness of a speech depends upon how well it is delivered to the audience. Have you ever observed how the meanings of a word or phrase can be altered just by the change of the tone of the voice and the body gestures? This is exactly what happens when a speech is presented.

The eyes of the audience remain focussed on the speaker from the moment the name is announced. The audience hears the introduction eagerly to find out how well the speaker is qualified to speak to them. They notice how he sits, how he walks to the lectern, stands, handles the mike and the posture he adopts when speaking. He is under the scrutiny of the audience.

Just as important as the wordings of the opening remarks is the way the speaker puts them across to the audience. The eye contact and the rapport the speaker establishes with the audience helps create a special relationship between the two. An audience is like a car. You start the delivery in the first gear, and move to second, third and the top gears. The speech catches up slowly. Having a message for the audience is necessary, but equally important is the enthusiasm the speaker has for the cause he presents. If the delivery lacks enthusiasm and sincerity the message cannot be effective. The audience will see through it. Enthusiasm is contagious. The speaker must be able to inject it into the audience. When the enthusiasm builds within the audience, the time is ripe to make the closing remarks and put forward a challenge to the audience to act.

According to Kenneth McFarland, "The best delivery is one that lets the audience concentrate exclusively upon *what* is being said, rather than *who* is saying it, or *how* it is being said."

Leon K. Whitney says, "Effective delivery is that in which every action so definitely adds to the effectiveness of the ideas expressed that the hearer is not conscious of delivery at all."

This is not as easy as it sounds. It requires practice, some more practice, and still some more practice. Speaking skills develop slowly. One of the most important elements of a good delivery is control over the voice. This comes with voice training. Just as singers train the voice through practice, public speakers too need to practice. The speaker needs to have a feeling for words. These feelings are eventually conveyed to the audience.

TRAINING THE VOICE

It is often asked when can a voice be called good. A good speaking voice is one that can be clearly and easily understood. It should not have any unpleasantness that detracts a person from what is being said. Some voices are high in pitch. Others are medium and a few are low pitched. The higher and medium pitch voices have better carrying power.

New comers can train their voice by reading loudly. Initially, they can read from a book or a magazine. They can then move on to read speeches by eminent speakers. Try to appreciate the words. Try to experience the feelings they convey. Soon you will be able to pass on these feelings to others. That is the time you will experience what effectiveness in speaking means.

Here are a few hints on voice improvement:

- If there is a speech defect consult a doctor. Many defects can be corrected.
- When you stand to speak, stand with confidence. Use nature's buoyancy and vitality to generate enthusiasm.
- Breathe naturally, deeply and often. Draw as much air into the lungs as possible.
- Relearn to use your vocal cords. Speak naturally.
- Project your voice by speaking to an object some distance away from you.
- While speaking give special emphasis to phonetics. Pronounce words correctly.
- Never copy someone else's voice or style.
- Be your own critic. Record your speech. How does it sound? Practice until you are satisfied.

Think it over...

The language of the heart, which comes from the heart and goes to the heart – is always simple, graceful, and full of power, but no art of rhetoric can teach it. It is at once the easiest and most difficult language, - difficult, since it needs a heart to speak it; easy, because its periods though rounded and full of harmony, are still unstudied.

— *Bovee*

HOLDING THE AUDIENCE INTEREST

It might be possible for the speaker to draw the attention of the audience through an attractive opening sentence. It might also be possible for the speaker to have a great message for the audience. But holding the interest of the audience throughout the presentation may not be easy.

This can be better understood when you observe the speaking and listening patterns in individuals. A person normally speaks at the rate of 125 -150 words per minute. On the other hand, a person is capable of listening at the rate of 600-700 words per minute. This means that a person can hear almost four times of what is being said by the speaker. With only one-fourth of the hearing capacity used, the listener's mind drifts to other thoughts. Questions pertaining to the speaker's message may emerge from these thoughts. This encourages a listener to interrupt the speaker, or ask questions. Since this is not possible during formal speeches, the listener observes some self-control, but nonetheless the mind drifts to other things.

Under such circumstances it becomes necessary for the speaker to make an extra effort to hold the interest of the listener. To make this possible, speakers use several techniques like changing the pace, adding some humour to the presentation, or telling an anecdote, using drama or modulations of the voice. These keep the listener involved in what is being said and prevents his thoughts from drifting. The use of these techniques requires practice. Some speakers tend to use them excessively, taking the attention away from the main subject of the presentation. A balance is necessary.

USING HUMOUR

Humour is very useful in drawing the immediate attention of the audience, to illustrate situations, change the pace of the speech and to help reach positive conclusions. Those who know how to use humour are remembered for their presentations. However, the use of humour is particularly difficult. Telling a funny story is not easy. Besides, everyone does not enjoy a similar level of sense of humour. A wrong use of humour can "switch off" the audience. Here are a few hints on using humour:

- Humour must be handled with care.
- Do not tell stories pertaining to religion, politics, racism or dialects. Someone in the audience can be sensitive to them.
- The story must be short and crisp. The audience thirsts for a witty punch line.
- Use humour as a tool to achieve your purpose, and not as a part of the subject of the speech.
- Use humour naturally without making the audience conscious of it.

USING VISUALS

Visuals have the ability of holding the attention of the audience better than the spoken words. It is for this reason that visuals are becoming popular in training presentations. Technological advances are to be seen in this field. From using flip charts, overhead projectors and slide projectors speakers are now freely using laptops and LCD projectors when making presentations. These have wide possibilities. The use of visuals and speech together not only helps hold the attention of the audience, but also makes the presentation very effective. It is now becoming commonplace to prepare presentations on the laptop.

CORRECT USE OF MIKE

For any presentation to be effective, it is necessary that the mike must be correctly used. In the majority of cases the mike is fixed on the lectern, or close to it so that the speaker can speak into it. As long as the speaker speaks directly into the mike, the sound is balanced. However, when a speaker moves to create an eye contact with the two ends of the audience, it is likely that the sound level may rise or fall, creating an unpleasant reaction, and adversely affecting the effectiveness of the presentation.

The quality of public address systems is likely to vary from one meeting to another. The acoustics of the meeting hall are also subject to various factors. These are not within the control of the speaker. He will need to make adjustments according to his need. The best a speaker can do is to be conscious that the public address system can make or mar the presentation, and in the interest of making the presentation effective the mike must be judiciously used.

INTERACTION WITH AUDIENCE

Experience has shown that whenever it is announced that there would be a question and answer session at the end of the presentation, the audience not only pays greater attention to the speaker, but also has questions ready to be asked. Many compete with each other to be the first to ask questions.

There are two reasons for the audience to ask questions. The first one is that they want a particular doubt clarified. The second one is that many in the audience want to test the speaker's knowledge and ability. Either way, the eye contact and the rapport between the speaker and the audience work effectively.

In training programmes the organisers cannot afford to have the attention of the participants deviate from the subject at hand. To overcome this problem, the training sessions are so organised that the speeches are limited, and there is greater interaction between the speaker and the audience. In such situations the speaker does not take chances, and to control the attention of the audience asks lead questions and asks different people to give a response to them. This way the audience cannot divert the attention to anything else. Provided the speaker is well informed and prepared, interactive sessions are always useful and effective in getting the message to the right people.

POINTS TO PONDER

- The speaker must understand the audience before he can speak to them.

- To succeed the speech must have a definite purpose.

- Speaking in excess of the allotted time can take the lustre off a good speech.

- Prior preparation is the backbone of an effective speech.

- An attractive opening is as good as half the speech.

- The body of the speech must elaborate on the purpose of the speech.

- The closing must tell the audience what is expected of it.

- The voice can always be trained for better performance.

- A good speaker holds the attention of the audience throughout the speech.

- Correct use of the mike and visuals enhance the effectiveness of the presentation.

- Audience participation adds to the effectiveness of the presentation.

Step
5

Pitfalls to Avoid

Public speaking is not without problems that one has to encounter. There is an old belief: If anything can go wrong, it will. This is true of public speaking more than anything else. The best of speakers have encountered situations that could not be avoided. They had to go through the experience any way. Their success at that time did not depend upon their speaking skills alone, but rather on how well they could manage the problem related to the place and occasion.

What kind of problems should a public speaker anticipate? New aspirants ask this question frequently. The answer is simple. Anything and everything is possible. There have been occasions when a speaker reaches the venue to find that the meeting has been cancelled, or the programme has been altered. The organisers may be there, but the expected audience has yet to assemble for one reason, or another. The speaking slots in the programme may have been changed without thought to continuity of subject or content.

At times the organisers may not have realised that the acoustics of the hall are not good. In such circumstances the audience cannot enjoy the best of speakers. The lectern may be ill designed. There have been occasions when a person standing behind the lectern is not visible to the audience. This means there is no eye contact between the speaker and the audience. There have been other occasions when the public address system is defective. Speakers have had to opt to speak without the mike. It is not unusual for an electricity failure to disturb a speech midway. It may take some time before the backup comes into operation.

AVOIDING PITFALLS

The best way to avoid the common pitfalls is firstly to anticipate them, and secondly to so prepare that they do not occur. A careful person is the best safety device.

Many public speakers argue that it is the responsibility of the organisers to ensure that all the physical arrangements are in order. If they go wrong, why should the speaker be perturbed? This might be true. However, after the speaker has put in effort to prepare a speech, if it fails even for no fault of the speaker, the failure would still affect the reputation of the person.

Many speakers are proactive and advise the organisers on matters like hall acoustics, sitting arrangement, placement of the lectern, the quality of the public address system, arranging an appropriate head-table and a backup in the event of power failure. Advising the organisers on these issues makes them aware of the basics of a good programme. Ultimately, it helps in reaching the message of the speaker to the audience.

PHYSICAL ARRANGEMENTS

A speaker cannot possibly have control over the physical arrangements at a meeting particularly so of the sitting arrangement, the hall acoustics or the control of the meeting programme even though these factors can enhance or diminish the speaker's effectiveness. However, the speaker can check the lectern and the passage leading to it. If the lectern is high, and the speaker is not tall enough to be able to see the audience from behind it, he can ask the organisers to have a podium to stand on. In the alternative, the speaker can also opt to speak by standing in clear view of the audience without using the lectern.

The passage to the lectern must be clear. If flower displays obstruct the passage to the lectern, these can be re-arranged to keep the passage clear.

The placement of the mike is important. Can it be adjusted for tall and short persons? Is it firmly fixed, or can it topple over? If a question and answer session has to follow the presentation, are the mikes correctly placed for the audience to access? Are there enough mikes? Is there a battery backup for the public address system? A little care to these arrangements ensures an effective meeting.

Think it over...

For want of a nail the shoe was lost; for want of a shoe the horse was lost; and for the want of a horse the rider was lost: being overtaken and slain by the enemy, all for want of care about a horse-shoe nail.

— *Benjamin Franklin*

PHYSICAL FAILURES

It may happen rarely but there have been occasions when temporary stages have caved in, vases toppled over, mikes overturned, and steps leading to the stage and the lectern collapsed. These instances evoke laughter in the audience, but create confusion for the organisers. The attention that was due to the speaker is diverted elsewhere.

In these circumstances the speaker needs to maintain his cool. Whatever has happened cannot now be avoided. The situation can only be corrected, and this too only within limits. There are no ready-made solutions. Every situation will need a different treatment.

If the stage is defective, a head-table can be arranged on the floor. If a vase or mike has overturned, they can be corrected. Apologies can be offered for the inconvenience caused. The situation must be handled expediently. The audience must appreciate that whatever could be done has been done.

FAILURE OF THE PUBLIC ADDRESS SYSTEM

The public address system fails rarely, but there are instances when it does happen. What has happened earlier can happen again. The present day public address systems are hi-tech and many of the earlier shortcomings have been taken care of. To ensure uninterrupted power supply backups can be installed. With all the care, what should be the speaker's reaction if the public address system fails midway in the programme?

The foremost thing to remember is: Do not panic. You may not be able to make the rest of the speech as effectively as you may desire to, but your presence of mind and a positive temperament can greatly salvage the situation. Do not stop the presentation. Make it look like a practical joke. "What a practical joke? Is this what they call 'There's many a slip between the cup and the lip'? Just when I had an important thing to tell you, the system has failed. Will we let this discourage us? Perhaps I need to speak a bit louder to reach you?"

You could at this stage leave the lectern and move closer to the audience to be better heard. If you were using notes, you will be at a disadvantage. You will now need to be concise and to the point. Go ahead and complete your talk without the audience knowing that you have had to cut out a part of it. Your handling the situation with a cool mind will help you win the confidence of the audience and the organisers.

POWER FAILURE

This problem was not common earlier. However, with the power crunch, when this problem will occur, it is difficult to tell. The organisers have no way to handle the situation completely. The obvious remedy is to have backup arrangements. When the power supply fails, the generators are switched on. If the backup system is automatic, there will be no break. However, when the generator has to be manually started there is bound to be a short break. When the generator is switched on another problem that may emerge is the sound of the generator unless it is enclosed, or placed at a distance from the meeting site.

On many an occasion it has been observed that when there is a sudden blackout, the speaker making a speech also suffers a blackout. The audience can appreciate that the speaker and the organisers are not to blame for the situation. Nonetheless it is a critical situation. What does the speaker do? Walk back to his seat? What happens to the programme?

Once again, it is the speaker who needs to maintain his cool. He was speaking when the power failed. He will need to adopt an attitude similar to the one he would on the occasion of the failure of the public address system. The attention of the audience has suddenly shifted from the speech to the blackout, and he will need to get it back. He will need to do some quick thinking, continue speaking, wrapping it up as best as he can to keep the audience involved. To be able to do this, it is essential that the speaker must always be well prepared for emergencies.

LOSING THE AUDIENCE CONFIDENCE

Even when every physical arrangement is in order and the audience is receptive, the speaker can still easily lose the confidence of the audience. This could be due to his attitude towards the audience. It could also be because of what the speaker has said. The audience may be "put off" by the remarks. Here are a few common causes that "turn off" the audience.

BEING APOLOGETIC

Have you noticed how many people stand up not to speak what they are expected to, but tell you, "The subject is so vast, but the organisers have allotted me only five minutes to speak. Is it possible to cover the subject in such a short time? I do not think so. However, I will try to do my best." How do you expect the audience to react to that? In their minds they have only one thought, "If you feel that you cannot cover the subject in five minutes, why are you speaking anyway?" The speaker has sent a wrong message even before saying a word on the subject. As it is, the speaker may already have lost a minute offering apologies even before he set out to speak on the subject.

Some more begin by saying, "I am not learned enough to speak before such a knowledgeable audience. The organisers have insisted that I must speak to you on the subject. I am not too sure, but still I will place before you whatever I do know." How will the audience react to this one? They will simply react, "If you do not know what you are talking about why did you agree to speak at all?"

There are others who will apologise for coming late, telling you about traffic jams and inefficiency of the traffic police. They will blame everyone, but would not tell you that they left home late. The audience reaction is that if he cannot manage himself, whatever can he tell us? He is not worthy of providing any useful information. The speaker is lost even before he has begun his speech.

Another common cause of apology is the time that has been allowed to the speaker to prepare the presentation. The speaker will begin by telling the audience that the time for preparation was too short. It was not possible to prepare the presentation well. The obvious audience reaction is that if you did not have time to prepare, you have no business to be wasting the time of the audience. You should speak only when you are well prepared.

There can be many excuses. The ineffective speakers use them as crutches. However, crutches cannot be hidden. They are there for everyone to see. The audience will always react to them in a negative way. A person who uses crutches is handicapped, and a handicapped person has no reason to tell an able person how to conduct himself. If you look back at the excuses, you will observe that had they been avoided, and the speaker would have spoken what he had to, the audience would have judged him or her on the basis of the presentation, and not on the basis of what went wrong where.

USING JARGON

Jargon refers to words and expressions used by particular groups. These are difficult to understand by persons who do not belong to that group.

It is not unusual for persons involved in specialized fields to use a lot of words and expressions that do not make any sense to the average person. This really means that the speaker is not aware of the lack of understanding for these terms by the audience. If the recipient of some information is ignorant of the terminology used by the person providing it, one should not be surprised when the communication fails.

It would be all right if a doctor was addressing a medical conference and talked of "carcinoma of the colon". However, if he used this terminology before a mixed group of people, it would not be surprising if they do not understand it even though the terms are simple and used in everyday medical discussion. The audience would appreciate and understand it immediately if the doctor talked of 'cancer of part of the large intestine'. In the same way, the doctor would not be easily understood if he talked of the patient suffering from "asphyxia". The average person would understand it immediately if the doctor used the word "choking" to describe the condition.

Doctors are not the only persons who use jargon when talking to others. In every field we find experts, particularly senior personnel who have been using these terms over a long period. Professors in different fields are particularly guilty of this fault. They are invited to speak to audiences at clubs and conferences because of their specialized knowledge, and they commit the fault of using this terminology. Later, they wonder why the information they provided was not well received. The next time you need to make a presentation make sure that you do not use "jargon", which the audience would fail to understand.

Think it over...

Say nothing of yourself, good, bad or indifferent; nothing good, for that is vanity; nothing bad, for that is affectation; nothing indifferent, for that is silly.

It is equally a mistake to hold one's self too high, or rate one's self too cheap.

— *J.W. Goethe*

SELF-IMPORTANCE

Just as there are people who lack the confidence to speak before an audience, there are others who, without being aware of it, feel excessively 'self-important'. These people love to praise themselves. They will tell you how as a child they could count up to 100 when their classmates could only count till 10. They will also tell you how they could form sentences when other children were struggling with the alphabet. They will remind you repeatedly about their superior education, about their performance at work and how they are respected by the society. Their family is no less exceptional. At 18 the wife was crowned the "Queen of the Hills", the daughter is growing up to be another beauty. The son is admired for his athletic skills. Everything about these people is very special. These people are always on an ego trip.

When these people stand up to speak before an audience their egos betray them. They tend to indulge more in self-praise rather than in conveying their message. How does the audience respond? They say, "If you are so special, how does that affect me? Can you help make me special? Of course, you cannot. So why should I care about what you have to say?" The audience is "switched off", and the speech falls flat. Many a presentation has failed because of the false sense of importance conveyed by the speaker.

TALKING DOWN

Most speakers are sensible not to adopt an attitude of self-importance. However, some use another technique to feel important. They talk down to people. Such speakers abound amongst the politicians. They have a keen observation. Unfortunately, the observation is lopsided. They only see one side of the coin, the shortcomings, and never the strengths. They are always looking for shortcomings amongst others. The moment they spot one, they are ready to talk about it in their speech. They will never tire of it. They can repeat it every time they speak. It is commonplace to hear politicians speak about the corrupt and immoral lives of their opponents. There might be a little truth in what they say, but just a pinch of salt and spice helps magnify and sensationalize the truth.

Talking down to people might provide some colour to common everyday gossip. However, when this is done in a formal speech before an audience, it is not appreciated in the least. In any audience the opinion of people is bound to be different. Talking down encourages whispering in the audience. They are soon "put off". The presentation fails to impress. It is necessary that every speaker must ensure that even if he or she knows about the shortcomings of their opponents, the facts will not be used in a formal speech before the public.

DIRTY JOKES

It is common for men and women to pass on dirty jokes in their own groups. Within these groups some take these jokes as humour, but quite a few even disapprove of them. In public speaking dirty jokes are taboo.

A few speakers argue that one should not be a hypocrite to laugh at a dirty joke in private, but frown at it in public. How does one differentiate between a joke and a dirty joke? At what point can a joke be described as dirty? In public speaking, propriety of conduct is important. Nothing should be spoken that would embarrass anyone, even on the pretext of humour. A joke becomes dirty when it causes embarrassment even if only to a few. Jokes can touch the sensitivities of some persons. When this happens, the speech fails to achieve its purpose. If one were not to achieve what one sets out to do so, why use dirty jokes? Why tread on a path that is uncertain?

Think it over...

Sarcasm is the language of the devil; for which reason I have long since as good as renounced it.

— *Thomas Carlyle*

SARCASTIC REMARKS

Similar to the use of dirty jokes a few speakers may make snide remarks as a measure to show disrespect or mock a person or a group. The speaker may comment that the remarks are intended to add a touch of humour, but the underlying desire may only be to mock or be sarcastic. It could also be said that the speaker is trying to "pull a fast one" in disguise. Such remarks are also referred to as "put-down", meaning a humiliating or critical remark. As long as a remark touches the sensitivities of some of the people in the audience it is not in good taste. Under such circumstances it should not be a part of the speech.

The use of such remarks is common amongst politicians. There have been occasions when these remarks had to be expunged from the proceedings in the parliament or legislative assemblies. Sometimes, to pacify provocations, apologies had to be tendered in public.

Some mischievous religious leaders are also in the habit of making remarks against groups following another faith or religious practices. At times these remarks have led to religious riots causing great damage to life and property. On every occasion a person speaking in public needs to be aware of public sentiments and emotions. An honest public speaker must be cautious about people's sensitivities and avoid untoward remarks.

USING FACTS AND FIGURES

A presentation is only as useful to the audience as the information they can remember and use in everyday life. When the speaker gives too many facts and figures in the speech, and the audience is unable to remember any of them simply because of the quantum of the information that has been conveyed is too large, the audience immediately "switches off".

The immediate reaction of the audience is that the speaker is aware that the information cannot be remembered. Knowing that it is not possible to remember so much data, when he includes it in the presentation, he does not want you to remember it. If it is not worth remembering, it is obvious that the other information provided by the speaker would also not be important to remember. Under such circumstances, why listen?

Whenever important facts are to be conveyed to the audience, and it is not possible for individuals to remember the details, it would be advisable to distribute a handout so that the audience can look over the figures and gauge the importance of the data at leisure. This way the message influences the audience better.

Another thing that can "switch off" the audience is when the speaker gives facts or figures that are not correct, are outdated and not reliable. It is not easy to get away with wrong information. In every audience there are people who are knowledgeable, and can pick out a discrepancy immediately. This makes it necessary for a speaker to research facts and figures correctly. With a lot of information available on the Internet this should not be difficult.

SMOKING AND DRINKING

It is not common for speakers to smoke and drink when making a speech. However, occasionally, at an informal dinner presentation or a group discussion a speaker may light a cigarette, or take a few sips from his glass. It is commonplace for smokers to light a cigarette when they need to think. They inhale deeply when in serious thought. Similarly, when the throat feels parched a few sips from the glass help speak smoothly.

Do not forget that when speaking the audience is not only hearing what the speaker is saying, but also observing how he or she is dressed, how he or she stands at the lectern, or what are the gestures one makes when speaking. Smoking or drinking may put the speaker to ease, but as gestures, they do not send out a positive message to the audience. A serious audience expects the speaker not to use smoking or drinking as crutches. It puts off the audience immediately. In the circumstances the presentation can never make an impact on the public.

Alcoholic drinks are sometimes used to combat stage fright. This can have a disastrous effect. Even very knowledgeable persons have been known to make a fool of themselves under the influence of alcohol. When a serious speech has to be made, alcohol is best avoided.

Travelling in a new country, Mark, a member of a study group was told by the leader that he would address the meeting of an elite group that evening. Having to speak before an audience that belonged to another culture made

Mark tense. To face the situation he compelled the hosts to provide him two bottles of beer. He guzzled them down to build courage to face the audience. The beer did not help much in adding to his confidence. With the increased liquid intake, Mark needed to leave the meeting thrice to visit the restroom. His nervousness was apparent. That left the visiting team and the audience greatly embarrassed.

SPEAKING IN EXCESS

Many people who have been speaking for a long time and are invited to address meetings make the common mistake of speaking in excess. Every programme allocates time for each item. The speaker is also advised how long he is expected to speak. Yet, feeling self-important, the speaker may go on speaking indefinitely. This only embarrasses the organisers and the audience. It does not matter how knowledgeable a speaker may be, one has no right to exceed the time allotted for the purpose.

The organisers always appreciate speakers who keep within the time allotted to them. This ensures a smooth programme with time for coffee breaks, or service of meals in time. The audience also appreciates speakers who keep to their time. One should not overlook that the receptivity of the audience is limited. They can hear for a certain time only. Once the receptivity falls, the speaker will never be appreciated. It is a rare speaker who can arouse such an audience.

You will notice that in schools and colleges the classes are limited to 40 to 45 minutes each. The specific reason for this is that it is not possible to hold the attention of the students beyond this time. The change of the subject and teacher offers a new interest. Keeping this in view, the organisers always plan a programme to hold the interest of the audience with a variety of items. To be appreciated by the audience, it is essential that the speaker must keep to time.

Think it over...

Every man must study conciseness in speaking; it is a sign of ignorance not to know that long speeches, though they may please the speaker, are the torture of the hearer.

— *Feltham*

LACK OF PREPARATION

Does it take long for the audience to realise that the speaker is not well prepared for the presentation? Of course not! The lack of preparation shows for itself. Some speakers, over-confident about their ability, will walk to the lectern without sufficient preparation only to find that making a formal speech is not as simple as they thought it would be. It can embarrass them, the audience and the organisers.

An important consideration is whether a speaker has the right to waste the time of the audience. Even if the speaker was to speak for 30 minutes to an audience of 20 persons, the immediate loss is 10 man-hours. Add to this, the time for formalities like introductions, commuting, waiting and thanksgiving, the loss of time would multiply. Even the most important of speakers have no right to waste the time of others.

The simple rule is: Be prepared or do not speak at all. It is true that it takes a lot of time to prepare for a presentation. Most speakers agree that it may take ten times as much in preparation as it would to speak. This would mean that for a 30-minute presentation it might take as much as five hours of preparation. The more experienced speakers take lesser time.

PRESENTING A WRITTEN SPEECH

A speaker who has a written speech may be confident that he has nothing to fear. All he has to do is just read out what is already written. No! Written speeches have every chance to fail to be appreciated by the audience.

Every presentation has three basic components. The speaker is the first part. He or she has a new set of ideas or information to present. The ideas or information that constitute the message form the second part of the process. The audience, as recipients of the message, forms the third part. For the communication to be successful all the three components must be in harmony. Even if one of the components is not so, the entire presentation can fail.

The speech must be well written. It must highlight the information that is to be conveyed. The language must be simple and convincing. It must gradually lead a person to act on what is being said. It is not sufficient that the speech is delightfully worded. The delivery of the speech by the speaker is very important.

Who has not seen speakers adjusting reading glasses trying to figure out a difficult word? Sometimes they try to connect the subject when a sentence is not read. It is also not uncommon for speakers to emphasize the wrong words or phrases. The worst that happens is that the speaker concentrates on the notes and fails to create an eye contact with the audience. The audience reaction is obvious. "If the speaker had to read out his speech, why did he not distribute a copy to each one of us? We could have read it at leisure, and also placed it on file for future use if it is relevant." Under these circumstances, can the speaker make an impact upon the audience? We see it happen every day.

When a speech is to be read by the speaker, it still requires a lot of preparation. Besides writing it well, the speaker needs to read it repeatedly until he has almost memorised it. The speaker must know what words and phrases need special emphasis. When the speaker is well acquainted with the written matter, he can raise his head periodically, look at the audience, smile and look around to create some eye contact. He can then come back to the speech. This shows that the speaker is as much concerned about the audience as he is about conveying the information.

Speakers who read speeches because there is no scope for deviation in language and words, and facts and figures of importance need to be cited, there is the need to develop techniques to do the job well. It requires both practice and patience. Only then can one expect a read out speech to influence the audience.

LACK OF COORDINATION

With the availability of a lot of aids that help put through a message more convincingly, many speakers are using these. However, one needs to remember that these aids do not in any way reduce the need for preparation for a formal presentation. It is true that many of these aids are very useful when correctly utilised. At the same time, if they are not correctly used, they are distractions the speaker is introducing between him and the audience.

On many occasions the speaker is able to create a good rapport with the audience, and the presentation goes on fine until the speaker, in his eagerness to show a couple of slides on the overhead projector draws the attention of the audience to the screen. The heads of the audience move, but unfortunately, the rapport between the speaker and the audience is broken. The speaker cannot establish the rapport again.

Many speakers are now using laptops and LCD projectors. The speaker must decide whether he wants the audience to look at him, or at the screen. They cannot surely look at both the places at the same time. Besides, there is always the danger that while shifting attention from one to the other, the attention may move to other thoughts.

To make good presentations, using the many aids that are now available, what is required most is good coordination. No aid can make up for the lack of ability. In every case, there is need for preparation and practice. Therefore, to succeed ensure that you are well prepared.

Think it over...

Never rise to speak till you have something to say; and when you have said it, cease.

— *Witherspoon*

POINTS TO PONDER

1. A public speaker has his share of problems to tackle.
2. A problem that is anticipated is a problem avoided.
3. When things go wrong the speaker must remain calm.
4. No pitfall could be as drastic as losing the confidence of the audience.
5. Never make up for personal shortcomings by offering apologies.
6. The use of technical jargon should be restricted to technical seminars and conferences.
7. The audience never appreciates a speaker who feels important, is sarcastic or talks down to others.
8. Never use dirty jokes or stories when speaking in public.
9. Facts and figures should be quoted only to exemplify a situation, and not to confuse it.
10. The feeling of confidence one experiences when smoking and drinking is illusory.
11. The audience immediately gets to know that the speaker is not prepared for the presentation.
12. Speeches that are read can fail as easily as other presentations.
13. Visual presentations must be well coordinated with the speech.

Speaking Aids

The layman will not immediately appreciate the kinds of aids that are available and used by speakers. Most people would think that all that a speaker needs are his notes, which he would have memorised and can dispense with. A large number of speakers generally speak loudly, and perhaps even the public address system could be eliminated unless the audience is big, and those sitting in the rear are unable to hear the speaker.

Have you ever observed a roadside salesman in the city? He walks over to the city square or a corner of the park, puts his things aside next to his assistant, places an old wooden crate in the centre, and using it as a podium to stand a wee bit higher begins to talk passionately. The passersby stop to watch what is going on. Slowly the crowd builds up. Soon there are enough prospective customers. The person now announces the magical benefits of what he is selling. Transactions take place between the assistant and the audience, as the speaker continues to beseech the passersby to join.

Things are rapidly changing. In a similar situation, the agents of a politician seeking election would also choose a spot in the city square or the park. Instead of the wooden crate serving as a podium, there would be a temporary stage. On the stage there would be banners in the backdrop, chairs for the speakers and also a lectern with several mikes and an efficient public address system. The organisers would play music and periodically make announcements about the arrival of the politician and other guest speakers. While the salesman is selling his ware, the politician is selling his services to the people of that constituency.

Public speaking is no longer a simple affair. Although the purpose is still the same – persuading people to buy products, services, information and ideas, the methods used aim at a higher level of effectiveness. The organisers are more concerned with making aids available, but the speakers need to know how to use them to be more effective. Some of the aids concern the speakers directly.

THE WHITE BOARD

A blackboard has always been one of the most elementary aids used by teachers in schools and colleges. To explain the subject, the teachers write on the blackboard with a white chalk stick. The writing stands out against the black background. In some places, the blackboard has given way to a green board. A more modern version is the white board that has a smooth writing surface. Special marker pens are used to write on them. Whereas black and green boards are still popular in schools and colleges because of the lower maintenance expenses, the more modern educational institutions and training centres run by corporate houses now use white boards, marker pens and special dusters.

White boards use laminated writing surfaces and are available in a variety of sizes. The laminated surface is being replaced with ceramic steel surface using newer technology that assures smoother writing, better chalk adherence, lesser chalk consumption and easier erasing with less chalk dust. These surfaces also provide increased colour contrast and reduced surface light distortion. This ensures optimum eye comfort.

A step ahead is the SMART Board, which serves as a huge computer screen and programmes are based on special software. These hi-tech boards have many possibilities including the access of websites and interactive use with the finger serving as the mouse.

FLIP CHARTS

A flip chart consists of a board that rests on a tripod stand with large flip chart pads fixed on the top of the board. The text is usually handwritten in large letters with marker pens. The writing is visible from a distance. The word flip chart is used because when the speaker has gone through one sheet, he 'flips' it over backwards to expose the next sheet. The word: chart is used because many speakers prepare graphics (charts) on these sheets for convenience of explaining the subject. These charts are not totally out of use, but serious speakers have moved on to sophisticated ways of making presentations.

Think it over...

Speech is silvern, silence is golden; speech is human, silence is divine.

— *German Proverb*

LECTERN

A lectern is a tall stand with a flat or sloping top on which the speaker can place written notes, using them as a guide, or even to read directly from them if the circumstances so require it.

A lectern is a great convenience aid for the speaker. It gives the person a place to keep the file or notes, and also covers the body of the speaker from direct view, thus protecting the speaker from misinterpretation of the body language by the audience. The lectern also provides the speaker space to place his hands and look directly at the audience.

Lecterns come in a variety of shapes and sizes. Unfortunately, all lecterns are not correctly designed. Many of them look artistic and grand, but are not comfortable for the speaker to use. Some are so huge that a person who is not tall is not visible to the audience in the front rows. Not being able to establish eye contact with the audience, the speaker is bound to be uncomfortable and upset. Under such circumstances it is best that the speaker use a podium to stand a few inches higher, or move out from behind the lectern to the open space so that eye contact can be established with the audience.

Some lecterns have an adjustable top for the convenience of the speaker. A few have a light fitted so that the speaker can read his notes. These lights can sometimes be adjusted to fall directly on the papers and not on the face of the speaker. A mike on a small stand can directly be placed on the lectern. This makes it easier to adjust by different speakers. The mike on a stand adjoining the lectern requires help to adjust, and is not convenient from the speaker's point of view.

In meetings where the audience is small, instead of a lectern, a small stand is placed on the table for the speaker to place and read notes standing behind the table. This is a makeshift lectern for the convenience of the speaker, particularly when the presentation has to follow a meal.

In churches, the lectern may be made of brass and is designed to hold the Bible. The minister can read directly during church service. Amongst the Sikhs, the Guru Granth Sahib is placed on a small cot, and supported with small pillows on both the sides. Hindus use a smaller wooden structure to place the Shrimad Bhagwat or the Ramayan, or other religious texts. In all cases, the purpose is to help provide support to the books or notes used by the speaker.

PODIUM

A podium is a small platform on which a person stands when conducting an orchestra, or giving a speech. The word 'podium' is often confused to mean a lectern. Many people use it to mean that. The word 'rostrum' is also used to mean a podium. The purpose of the podium is to help a speaker stand a little higher than the audience to enable an eye contact and establish rapport with them. When the lectern is high, or the speaker is short and is not visible from behind the lectern, it is commonplace to provide a podium to the speaker so that he or she stands higher, and there is clear visibility between the speaker and the audience. When organizing conferences where many speakers would be invited to speak, it is advisable to have a podium that can be used to provide speaking comfort to speakers who are not tall.

A popular use of the podium can be observed on sports fields where at the end of the race the first, second and third winners stand on to receive their medals.

DAIS

Dais is yet another word that is often misinterpreted to mean the head-table, or those sitting on the stage. Derived from the French language, dais is a low platform for placing a lectern or a throne. In colleges, the lecturer's table and chair is placed on a platform a few inches above the normal floor. This can be called a dais. It is intended to give the lecturer and the class to get a better view of each other.

PUBLIC ADDRESS SYSTEM

When an audience is small, a speaker can speak directly to be heard by everyone. However, when the audience is large, and it is not possible for the speaker to speak loud enough to be heard by those in the rear rows, it becomes necessary to make provisions for a public address system.

A public address system, popularly known as a PA system, is an electronic amplification device constituted of an amplifier, a mixer and loudspeakers. Sound goes to the amplifier through a microphone. Several kinds of PA systems are available in the market. They range from the small hand-held battery operated system that a person can easily carry and speak through in remote areas to sophisticated systems that have a power output for a person to be heard in a stadium occupied by 50,000 people. The small and medium sizes are used in halls and auditoriums where speakers are invited to speak.

The earlier models were not without problems, but with the present day hi tech products, the public address systems are easy to use and provide excellent sound amplification without any disturbance.

Corded mikes that are connected with the amplifier are commonly used, but equally popular now are cordless mikes that can be moved to different parts of the auditorium. These have greatly increased the effectiveness of presentations. A step still ahead for persons who would like to keep their hands free and still move through the audience, or not keep standing behind the lectern, there are collar mikes that can be clipped on to the dress or the coat collar.

A problem that needs the attention of the organisers pertains to the potential for "feedback" in PA systems. This occurs when the sound from the loudspeakers returns to the microphones, and is then re-amplified and sent to the speakers. This manifests as a sharp, screeching high-volume sound, which can damage the speakers. The solution lies in having correct acoustics and placement of loud speakers.

A subject closely related to PA systems is the need for good acoustics for a speaker to be heard clearly in a large hall. When designing auditoriums, engineers take special care in ensuring that the acoustics are right. Many meetings, even conventions, have failed because of poor acoustics. A speaker cannot do anything about the situation. However, he can understand that sometimes when a part of the audience fails to hear the cause could be poor acoustics of the hall.

Think it over...

If a man write a better book, preach a better sermon, or make a better mouse-trap than his neighbour, though he build his house in the woods, the world will make a beaten path to his door.

— *R. W. Emerson*

TELEPROMPTER

A teleprompter is a display device that prompts a speaker with an electronic visual text of the speech or script. The speaker reads directly from the text that comes before him without having to look at notes. This gives the impression that the speaker is speaking spontaneously.

This device dates back to almost 50 years when television performers needed to memorise large amounts of material, and there was not enough time for it. Even today, the device is most used in television studios where newsreaders read directly looking at the camera.

In the earlier models, the script was printed on a paper scroll, which was slowly advanced as the speaker read from it. To the audience it appeared that the speaker has memorised the speech and is speaking spontaneously. In television studios the 'teleprompter' was placed close to the camera.

From the speaker's point of view this is a great device because he can read the speech, and yet do it so naturally that it leaves a lasting effect upon the audience. This device is used by speakers in hi-tech training seminars and conventions. This eliminates the chances of the smallest mistake by the speaker that might create a wrong impression on the audience.

SCRIPTS AND NOTES

In technical conferences and training seminars it is usual for speakers to either bring the entire presentation in script form and read from it, or bring notes to guide them as they make the presentation. Circumstances and situations are bound to vary on different occasions. The speakers will need to make adjustments accordingly.

When the speaker is presenting technical information and data, and there is no scope for any omissions, the ideal situation would be to read out the speech. This can be monotonous to the audience, and their attention may drift away, making the presentation a futile exercise. The only solution lies in the ability of the speaker to use techniques to hold the attention of the audience.

Normally, most speakers are content when they carry notes that they use to ensure the correct point-by-point presentation. Some carry the complete script in a file that can be rested on the lectern. The speaker does not read the speech, but may refer to it occasionally to maintain continuity, and also read out "quotations" from other sources. The important thing is to maintain eye contact with the audience and also refer to the notes.

When the speaker is not speaking from behind a lectern and either standing before the audience, or moving amongst them, the notes are best made on cards, written boldly only on one side and correctly numbered to follow the subject sequentially. This requires a good knowledge and preparation by the speaker.

VISUAL PRESENTATIONS

We are repeatedly reminded that a good picture is worth a thousand words. A good public speaker is no less aware of it. Visuals are quick to draw attention. It is for this reason that speakers have used a variety of techniques to take advantage of this fact. Some of the earliest projectors were bulky and expensive. Over the years techniques have changed. New equipment has made it possible to present top quality presentations repeatedly.

OVERHEAD PROJECTORS

An overhead projector is a device that projects an enlarged image of a transparent photograph or gelatin slide, by means of an overhead mirror. The earlier models were bulky, but now sophisticated portable models are also available. This device is useful for teaching purposes when the audience is limited. The use is very simple. A prepared photograph or slide is to be simply placed on the flat well-lit surface. It is projected on the screen through an overhead mirror. The device requires minimal care and maintenance.

The slides can be prepared by composing the matter on a computer, and then printing them on a printer. It is also possible to write directly on these transparent sheets with a black pen. The slides could be printed black and white, or also in colour, depending upon the need.

Since each slide has to be manually placed and removed, the spontaneity of a presentation can be affected. To avoid this the speaker could have an assistant to change slides. While the assistant would place the slides, the speaker could continue speaking uninterruptedly so that the rapport that has been built with the audience may not be disturbed. Some speakers place the projector in such a way that they can change the slides and also keep speaking to the audience, sneaking a glance once in a while at the screen.

Think it over...

Eloquence is the transference of thought and emotion from one heart to another, no matter how it is done.

— *John B. Gough*

SLIDE PROJECTORS

A slide projector makes it possible to view photographic slides on a big screen. Initially, black and white slides were used. These were soon replaced by the colour slides. The earlier projectors were manual, and the slides had to be changed one after the other. As each slide was displayed the speaker gave the details verbally on a PA system if the audience was large. When the speaker was well prepared, the combination of visual presentation with a verbal commentary created an effective impression upon the audience.

The manually operated projectors were soon replaced with projectors that carried slide boxes that carried 36 slides at one time and could be moved with a remote button. The 36-slide cartridge was soon overtaken by an 80-slide round tray that also moved the slides through a remote. Excellent presentations were possible in colour. Since the projectors used photographic colour slides, they found great popularity in homes and clubs. The business utility was limited to viewing pictures of outstation projects and applications.

Slide projectors have a limited use now in schools to view colour slides about different subjects. The film cameras are gradually becoming obsolete. It is also not possible to have films processed and slides made because of lack of laboratories. Digital photography is gaining popularity. It is now possible to make colour prints at home. It is also possible to make changes on the computer screen. The images on the computer screen can now be directly viewed on a larger screen.

LCD PROJECTORS

An LCD projector has now replaced the overhead projector and the slide projector. This projector displays the computer screen directly on to a large screen or screens being viewed by a large audience. Since it is possible to view visuals, written matter, slides, video clippings and movies on a computer screen, it is simultaneously possible to view the same on a large screen through an LCD projector.

An LCD projector uses a halogen lamp as a light source. These lamps are capable of producing sufficient light to display a good image on the screen. The popular brands average between 2,000 — 4,000 ANSI lumens. Since the size of the projector is small, it is very easy to carry. A portable screen and the projector can be installed within a few minutes. In very large auditoriums it is possible to project on large fixed screens.

The LCD projector has made it possible to have comfortable home theatres. People view DVD quality movies on a large screen at home. Technologies are changing very rapidly. It is difficult to predict what to expect in the next few years.

Whatever preparation a public speaker can make on a computer can be used effectively when making a presentation before a large audience. The larger personal computer has been replaced with a handy laptop that has all the abilities of the larger model. This way it is now possible to have colour visuals in the form of slides and video clippings along with written notes written on the visuals. The speaker stands behind the lectern controlling the movement of the slides and visuals, speaking into the mike directly reading out the written material that appears on the laptop screen. While there may be no eye contact between the speaker and the audience, the audience looks at the large screens, as the speaker keeps them attracted by modulating his voice in harmony with the need, directly reading from the laptop screen. This makes the presentation colourful, alive and attractive. The secret of making it effective lies in preparing and rehearsing it well on the laptop.

A LAPTOP COMPUTER

With computers having gained mass acceptance as a vital communication tool in just a little over a decade, most of the earlier speakers did not have appropriate knowledge to modify their presentations. However, all the newcomers and also most of the old-timers now use laptops to prepare their presentations and carry these to the meeting. Even when not carrying a laptop, some of the speakers carry the presentation on a CD that can be used on another computer or laptop. This means that in future there will be a lot of hi-tech presentations.

PRESENTATION SOFTWARE

With computers and LCD projectors playing a key role in making presentations, it is essential that the person making the presentation must have knowledge of the software that is used to prepare these programmes. The most popular software used for the purpose is Microsoft PowerPoint. There are other software like OpenOffice.org Impress and Apple's Keynote.

Many of the presentation programmes come with clip art that can be used to prepare presentations. Some have the ability to import graphic images. Some speakers first prepare the graphics on programmes like Adobe Photoshop and Adobe Illustrator, and then import them to the presentation. With growth in digital photography and equipment, many options are opening up for speakers to prepare great presentations. It is also possible to add music to the presentation.

While great things are now possible with presentations, and individual creativity and imagination dictate the quality, it has simultaneously become necessary for the speakers to be well acquainted with the use of the new software, or to take support of others in making scintillating presentations.

> ## Think it over…
>
> The elegance of the style, and the turn of the periods make the chief impression upon the hearers. Most people have ears, but few have judgment; tickle those ears, and depend upon it, you will catch their judgments such as they are.
>
> — *Chesterfield*

MICROSOFT POWERPOINT

Microsoft PowerPoint continues to be the most popular presentation software. As a part of the Microsoft Office system it has achieved worldwide popularity. First introduced in 1990, the software has been upgraded periodically. It offers many facilities and changed the way speakers now plan their presentations. Even those who would have never thought of using visuals in their presentations are doing so now. It would be useful if speakers learn the use of this software to derive complete benefit of making effective presentations.

POINTERS

When a speaker uses visuals on a large screen there arises the need for explaining some points in detail. It becomes necessary to point out to a particular portion of the screen to draw the attention of the audience. It has been customary to use thin long pointers in training sessions. Since they come between the projection source and the screen they cause irritating shadows, and are best avoided. The modern way is to use a laser pointer, which is like a pen torch and projects a red dot that can be pointed at the exact point. It would be useful if the speaker carries one in his pocket.

A MODERN SETUP

An ideal modern setup for a speaker would include a lectern that is large enough to place a laptop computer with a connection for it to be joined to the LCD projector, a tabletop mike and a small timepiece to keep time. This would enable a quick changeover from one speaker to another. This means that the conventional lecterns will need to be modified. Care will also need to be exercised in placing a screen, or screens, depending upon the size of the audience.

ROOM SETUP

Most people would argue that the organisers are responsible for the room setup and not the speaker, but it is necessary that the speaker be acquainted with different kinds of room setup, and also that the setup can affect the effectiveness of the presentation.

At the lowest level a speaker may be expected to speak to a very small group seated around a round table. The atmosphere would be informal, and speaker could address the audience sitting, with notes on the table. When sitting, using the notes should be easy and comfortable.

When the audience is a little larger, say from 10 to 25 persons, the audience could be seated with tables and chairs arranged in U-shape. The speaker sits facing the 'U'. He can speak seated or may stand when speaking. This arrangement allows the speaker to maintain eye contact and rapport with everyone, facilitating informal discussions. The participants can respond to the speaker and also take notes. If required, a screen can be placed for visual presentations.

Another modification of the U-shape is the conference, or the closed square setup commonly used in the conference rooms of corporate houses. There is a long table with people sitting on three sides, and the speaker sits on one side. This way the speaker can address the participants as a whole, or have one-to-one discussion. For visuals a screen can be fixed within everyone's view behind the speaker.

There is yet another setup where the speaker and the organisers sit on the head table while the audience sits around round tables. The setup is popular when the speaker addresses a group assembled for a banquet. The speeches may be organised prior to the meal, or after it. In some cases, a part of the programme is conducted before the meal, and the closing remarks and thanksgiving follow the meal. Few people are attentive after a meal. Care must be taken that nothing is served during the programme or speeches. With waiters moving around the tables the effect of the presentations is totally lost.

A popular form of setup is known as the classroom setup. Just as in a class, everyone sits in rows facing the teacher's table occupied by the speaker. There is a passage between two blocks of rows. The speaker may write on a whiteboard, or may have a screen to project the visuals.

Another option of the classroom setup is when the rows are not straight as in a class, but for a better interaction with the speaker they are inclined with a passage in between the two blocks. This is known as the herringbone setup. When no tables are required, the chairs could still be arranged in a herringbone setup.

When the group becomes bigger, the tables in front of the participants are removed, and we have rows of chairs divided popularly into two blocks divided by a passage. This is known as the theatre setup. It is a popular setup when the audience is large. The speaker and the organisers would sit on a head table on a stage. The lectern too would be placed on the stage for easy visibility for the speaker and the audience.

The organisers invite a speaker to address the audience for a particular purpose. The speaker knows best how this purpose can be achieved. K eeping this in view, the speaker is within his rights to suggest whatever setup would be most suitable for the purpose.

Think it over...

Oratory, like the drama, abhors lengthiness; like the drama, it must keep doing. Beauties themselves, if they delay or distract the effect, which should be produced on the audience, become blemishes.

— *Bulwer*

PERSONAL NEEDS

Although many people are now using bifocal spectacles for convenience, many speakers use reading glasses. They can be uncomfortable without them. It is therefore advisable that they must carry one in their kit when going for a presentation. Removing the normal spectacles now and then to read or consult the notes can be distracting for the audience.

Most presentations are time bound. The organisers inform in advance as to the time that is allotted to the speaker. This will include the time required to place the laptop on the lectern and get it connected to the LCD projector. For a presentation to be effective it is necessary that the speaker must maintain the time schedule. To enable this a watch is necessary. Most speakers wear wristwatches. It is usual for most of them to take it off and place it on the lectern when they arrive to speak. They can keep an eye on the time, and yet the audience will not get to know it.

On some occasions, particularly during training seminars where the time schedules are very tight, and the organisers are particular that the message of excellent time management is inculcated in the minds of the participants, the organisers have time keepers sitting in the last row. Five minutes before the allocated time they will signal "5 Minutes Left". Using this as a cue the speaker can wind up the presentation.

It is common that when people speak continuously the mouth tends to dry up. With some people it is more compared to others. Under such circumstances a few sips of water help. Since asking for a glass of water in the middle of a presentation breaks the flow of thoughts, and can rob it of its effectiveness, it is necessary that if the speaker desires a few sips of water during the presentation, it must be requested for at the beginning of the presentation. The glass of water can be placed in a corner of the lectern, and used at personal convenience.

Since mucous collects in the throat and on drying creates irritation many speakers are compelled to clear the throat before speaking. A few sips of water or a cup of tea or coffee before the speech can be helpful. Some use peppermint or a piece of candy to keep the throat clear.

AUDITORIUM LIGHTS

The organisers normally look after the auditorium lights and the speaker has no control over them. However, if it is necessary to use visuals and projectors it would be necessary to dim the lights to improve the visibility of the screen. In that event it is necessary that the speaker must inform the organisers to have a person control the lights of the auditorium as and when required. This must be done in advance so that the audience may not notice it.

POINTS TO PONDER

1. In a classroom atmosphere speakers prefer to use whiteboards.
2. Lecterns come in a variety of shapes and sizes.
3. A podium is useful when the lectern is high and the speaker short.
4. A good public address system is necessary for an effective presentation.
5. A teleprompter is useful in large seminars, conferences and conventions.
6. A speaker learns to make notes according to personal style and need.
7. Visual aids are popular with many speakers. They need expert handling.

8. Knowledge of presentation software helps prepare effective presentations.

9. The room setup helps create rapport between the speaker and the audience.

10. The speaker must ensure personal needs are available.

Towards Greater Perfection

We are finally at the last step to becoming an effective public speaker. Over the past steps we have observed the importance of public speaking in everyday life, and also how the fear of speaking holds back the vast majority from making the effort. We have also learned about the essentials that help develop speaking skills, and how presentations can be effective. As in any other field, there are pitfalls to avoid. When we know about them there is no reason to get discouraged. We can always get over them. Besides, there are always the speaking aids that can be useful to any speaker aspiring to be recognised.

We are closing in towards the goal of becoming an effective speaker, but we are still not quite there. We need to persevere a little more. It is not enough to understand only the basics. We must know how good speakers perfect their presentations. We are aware of the great effort that goes into the preparation of each presentation. But how is it that speakers appear to do it effortlessly? Are they so blessed that they can make an extempore presentation at any time? Is that technique or experience? Can an average person also attain that level of competence? What does one need to do?

At every step it has been repeatedly said, "Effective public speaking is an acquired skill. Everybody can learn it." This is truth. All successful speakers would agree on it. Since every public speaking opportunity is different, once a person learns the basics, it is a matter of learning from every experience. Even when a person is not speaking and only listening to someone else speak, there is much to learn from the way speakers make presentations. Observe how they succeed. Also look for reasons when you notice someone slip. There are lessons to be learnt from successes and failures.

THE TIME FACTOR

Every good speaker needs to remember two important things:

1. To reach in time for a speaking assignment.
2. To restrict the speech to the time allotted for the purpose by the organisers.

Some speakers have the habit of reaching late expecting that the programme may begin late. Check the time with the organisers and ensure your presence accordingly. If you do not reach in time, the organisers would not invite you again. Besides, reaching late can be very embarrassing.

A politician had been invited to speak on the occasion of the retirement of a priest in the church. The priest had completed 25 years in service to the community, and the function had been organised in his honour. Unfortunately, the politician did not turn up on time, and the organisers decided to go ahead with the programme. They requested the priest to speak about his experience in the community.

The priest said, "When I came to this community 25 years ago I was shocked when on the first day a man came to make a confession. He said he had stolen a motorcycle, and when caught by the police he was able to deceive them. He had often stolen money from his parents and also cheated where he worked. He also confessed to have had an affair with the boss's wife. Shocked to hear the confession I told him that his having spoken the truth would unburden him from the sins he had committed. I did wonder if I had come to a wrong community. I soon found that my fears were misplaced because there were a lot of good people. I have been happy to be a part of the community."

Hardly had the priest said this much that the politician arrived and walked straight to the stage. The organisers asked him to take over.

"Friends," the politician said, "I am sorry for coming late. I was especially looking forward to speak on this occasion. In fact, when our priest arrived 25 years ago, I was the first person to have confessed to him."

The politician could not understand it but the audience broke into uncontrollable laughter.

READING A SPEECH

While it is common for academic papers to be read at workshops and conferences, it is equally common when ministers, statesmen, politicians and even senior executives read out speeches written by learned persons. Reading a speech or a report or information is speaking in public, but not what is understood by the term 'public speaking'. Written information is hard, cold facts. The interest of the audience in facts is limited to information that is of immediate use to them, not just any kind of information. This means that the facts must touch their everyday life, or their hopes and aspirations. This does not always happen. Therefore, one should not be surprised when a speech falls flat.

Why is it that a speech written by a learned person fails to hold the attention of the audience? The answer is very simple. The information being conveyed to the audience is only a part of the communication. To be effective, the speaker must have a personality in harmony with what is being conveyed. Without it he or she will not be able to attract the attention of the audience. Next, the person must be able to hold the attention of the audience. The quality of the voice and the delivery are very important. It is also necessary that the audience must be receptive to what is being conveyed by the speaker.

To be effective, the experienced public speaker moulds the sentences to a language he or she is well acquainted with. The audience is not concerned how learned the person whose thoughts are being delivered is in real life. The audience wants to hear a new and better version of what is already known about the subject. This is where the public speaking skills really work. A good public speaker must present very simple ideas in an interesting manner.

Here are a few tips for an effective presentation:

- Be relaxed. You speak better when you are relaxed.
- Breathe deeply. The additional oxygen adds to your confidence.
- Be prepared. Good preparation promotes self-confidence.

- Practice before you make a preparation.
- Believe in what you are going to speak. There is a connection between what you feel and what you speak.
- Speak naturally as you would to friends.

Think it over...

Although there are certain things, such as pauses, breathing, and pitch of voice, that are very important, none of these can take the place of *soul* in an address.

— *Booker T. Washington*

PURPOSE OF THE PRESENTATION

Unless a presentation has a purpose it cannot succeed. No amount of knowledge can carry one through. When there is no purpose, there is nothing to achieve. When there is nothing to achieve, a speech is no more than filler in the programme. Filler has no other purpose than to be a time cushion. No accomplished speaker would opt for such an assignment.

A speech can have one of the following three purposes:

1. To inform the audience about something.
2. To get the audience to act about something.
3. To entertain the audience.

The purpose to inform is a popular reason for speeches in schools, colleges and universities, at the workplace and at a whole lot of other places. The primary purpose is to share information or knowledge. When the purpose of the speech is to make the audience act, the speaker is really trying to sell an idea or a product. One may succeed at the first attempt. Generally, a seed of the idea is sown in the mind of the audience and a final response follows later. Entertainment is a specialised field, and does not come strictly within the scope of public speaking. Specialists in this field share the stage with others in the field, and appear at live performances and television shows for purposes of entertainment only.

Although the three purposes of a presentation have been identified, in actual practice it is to be observed each of them overlap. If one were to analyse some of the speeches one would observe that speakers simultaneously inform, entertain and ask the audience to act. Nonetheless it is very important that the speaker must keep the purpose of the presentation in mind.

How important is the purpose of the presentation? We discussed this earlier. The truth is that having a purpose for a presentation is more important than some of the basic elements of public speaking discussed earlier. A definite purpose outweighs all of them. Who has not heard of Mahatma Gandhi, Mother Teresa, Helen Keller, Billy Graham or Nelson Mandela? They had purposes taller than all the principles of public speaking. The audience did not care about their body language or the voice quality. At every opportunity the audience thronged to hear the 'message' they had for the common man. Their sincere concern for mankind has left an indelible impression in the minds of people wherever they went. It can be said that the audience is willing to hear speakers who are sincere, and practice what they preach.

Think it over...

Courage, endurance, fearlessness and above all self-sacrifice are the qualities required of our leaders. A person exhibiting these qualities in their fullness would certainly be able to lead the nation, whereas the most accomplished orator, if he has not these qualities, must fail.

— *Mahatma Gandhi*

LEADERSHIP AND PUBLIC SPEAKING

We have just observed that the audience was always willing to hear Mahatma Gandhi, Mother Teresa and others because of the message they conveyed. At the same time we cannot overlook that all of these persons possessed leadership qualities. As leaders they stood high above others. All of them had risen above their personal needs, made outstanding sacrifices and above all else thought from the point of view of the common man.

The leader leads by example, not by speech. Therefore, if the speaker wants to be effective in making the audience act on the proposed idea, the audience must be convinced that the speaker has already put into practice what he wants them to do. An audience is always willing to follow an accepted leader. Even if the speaker is new to the audience but his credentials highlight leadership characteristics, the audience will find it easier to accept him and his suggestions. Leadership and public speaking are closely linked. A leader has good speaking skills, and to be effective a speaker must possess leadership qualities.

Sincerity is a salient quality in every leader. It emerges from one's conscience and immediately bridges the gap between what one says and what one does. One cannot pretend to be sincere. The audience can see through it. The inner sincerity shows as body language, and sends out positive signals to the audience to accept what is being said.

It would not be enough for an aspiring speaker to learn only the basics of public speaking. To be effective the speaker will need to develop the entire personality to fulfil the role of a model person who can inspire and motivate the audience by the example of personal life. Just as the personality develops, one can use speaking skills with greater authority.

SIMPLICITY IN SPEAKING

Have you ever noticed that each of the leaders and acclaimed speakers we discussed were known to speak a very simple language? This is a prized quality in every effective public speaker. Irrespective of how difficult or complicated a problem may be, a good speaker presents it to the audience in the simplest of words so that a person with an average knowledge and ability can also understand it. This makes it easier for the audience to understand the problem and also find suitable solutions.

Simplicity of thinking and action comes from an above average knowledge and vision of the subject. A newcomer may not understand it. It is only through thorough knowledge and deep inner thought that a person is able to simplify the subject. Simplification helps in finding solutions and turning thoughts into actions.

A good public speaker should be like a schoolteacher who simplifies everything for the student to grasp the concept of the subject. A good teacher helps associate new information and knowledge with what the student already knows. It is important that everyone in the audience must understand what the speaker is trying to convey. Only then it would be accepted and acted upon. It has been observed that 95% of the words used by effective speakers are of one or two syllables. The rest are three syllable words. This takes us back to an earlier lesson that good speakers use simple words and short and easy sentences. Simplicity is the key to making a presentation effective.

PREPARATION

An able speaker puts in a lot of effort into a presentation so that it may appear to be effortless. Nothing has ever been achieved without an effort. It is also true that the results of effort may not be visible immediately, but no effort was ever been wasted. The results accumulate and show up later.

We examined President Abraham Lincoln's address at Gettysburg. Observing the length of the address anyone would readily believe that the President prepared it on his way to Gettysburg. However, his companions confirmed that he did not touch pen or paper on the way. There is evidence that some of the phrases were coined months before the address. It only proves that the problem had been in the President's mind and he was toying with the words months before he actually spoke them. Such was his preparation.

An able speaker is not a con man that talks the audience into action. The speaker is able to persuade the audience to act because of the knowledge of the subject, the research and preparation. A well-prepared speaker is ready for all kinds of situations during the presentation. The message is backed up with reason and logic. The audience can see the sincerity in the speaker's eyes. The concern is clearly visible. In such circumstances would they not be motivated? It is a win-win situation for both the speaker and the audience.

PREPARATION TECHNIQUES

No two persons are alike. In the same way no two speakers present the subject in the same way. Every speaker develops a style over a period. While a speaker who opts for the field of entertainment is oriented towards laughter and the lighter side of life, speakers who inform, sell and motivate use a variety of methods to touch the sensitivities of the audience.

An able speaker understands that the mind of the audience is fickle. On the slightest pretext it moves from one thought to another. The rapport between the speaker and the audience can break at any time. To prevent this from happening speakers use a variety of techniques like making sensational statements, telling a story or anecdote, quoting from religious scriptures, drawing upon an incident in personal life or using humour to keep everyone attracted.

During the speech it appears that the speaker has just remembered something and decided to narrate it.

However, all speakers are known to prepare the "spontaneous reactions" earlier, and also rehearse them before the presentation. This is important because a joke can fall flat if the speaker does not know how to present it. In a story or anecdote the speaker must know what to emphasize. The inclusion of these should enable the speaker to carry forward the audience towards attaining the purpose of the speech.

In adopting presentation techniques and style every person must keep one's personal temperament in mind. Everyone is not a good storyteller just as everyone cannot tell a good joke. There are some who have their arsenals loaded with stories and jokes, but most follow a middle path and blend different techniques to keep the presentation in harmony with the personality.

FLEXIBILITY

All speakers need to be flexible. Have you ever observed how a novice gets disturbed when he is asked by the organisers to cut short his presentation because of paucity of time? When asked to speak for 5 minutes instead of the 10 minutes allotted to him earlier, he doesn't know what part of the presentation can be avoided.

In the same way, have you observed how a speaker does not know how to handle the situation when he is asked to follow a very eloquent speaker who had the audience enthralled and received great applause?

In such a situation when a person was asked to thank the speaker, to match the eloquence of the speaker who had earlier complimented the audience by repeatedly calling it 'charming', the person entrusted with the thanksgiving walked confidently to the lectern and said,

"When the chief guest speaker like the one we have today is very learned and eloquent, there could be no better way to thank him than to steal his own words and say, 'what a charming guest speaker we have this morning'." The speaker and the audience were taken aback by the remark and broke into laughter. The rest was easy. The person heartily accepted the challenge the speaker had placed before them. The audience applauded a spontaneous acceptance. The purpose was achieved.

It is not unusual when several speakers speak one after the other, though for short periods, a speaker may suddenly get stuck when an earlier speaker has raised the same points that he was going to talk about. On one occasion, finding him in such a dilemma a speaker said, "Do you know why Sam wanted to speak before me? He stole my speech." The audience laughed. The speaker went on to salvage the situation.

In a moment of crisis humour is useful. However, just as everyone cannot tell a joke well, everyone cannot use humour well.

We have earlier discussed possible pitfalls. To be appreciated, a public speaker must know how to change course midway when a problem raises its head. Flexibility is important. Ready solutions cannot be suggested. Every situation is unique. One will have to address it on the spur of the moment.

VISUAL SUPPORT

Visuals always create an immediate impact on the audience. Speakers who are good photographers are known to have used colour slides in their presentations. OHPs made presentations easier for technical and training seminars. In the last decade the use of computers and LCD projectors changed the way important presentations were made. With the coming of laptop computers and new software public speaking is becoming hi-tech.

Instead of carrying notes it is now possible to have the entire presentation on a laptop computer. New technology does not create an impact by itself. It requires as much preparation as was required earlier. Only the kind of preparation has changed. The selection of visuals and words is just as important as it always was. Many eager enthusiasts have rushed into becoming hi-tech speakers, but without sufficient knowledge and technique many presentations have fallen flat. For example, spelling mistakes in notes would go unnoticed because words are being spoken only. When you put words or phrases on visuals you are under the scanner for mistakes.

The visibility of the screen is an important consideration. Is the screen large enough for all the audience to see it? Are the words on the visuals large enough to be read from every point in the auditorium? Since everything cannot be written on the visuals it is important that the speaker must be well rehearsed with the matter that is being spoken. Coordination between the visuals and the spoken part is important for a presentation to be effective.

Since visuals are not required for every presentation an important consideration for a speaker is whether to use visuals or to speak directly to the audience. Speaking directly to the audience has its own advantages in that the speaker is able to make eye contact and establish rapport with the audience. The gestures influence as much as the words. He is able to get a feedback through their expressions. When visuals are used the eyes of audience remain focussed on the screen, and not on the speaker.

> ## Think it over...
>
> Extemporaneous speaking is, indeed, the groundwork of the orator's art; preparation is the last finish, and the most difficult of all his accomplishment. To learn by heart as a schoolboy, or to prepare as an orator, are two things, not only essentially different, but essentially antagonistic to each other; for the work most opposed to an effective oration is an elegant essay.
>
> — *Bulwer*

SPEAKING EXTEMPORE

Extempore speaking is understood to mean speaking without preparation. At the same time speaking impromptu means speaking without a plan or preparation. Speaking spontaneously means speaking on a sudden impulse, obviously without preparation. The three words have similar meanings, but strictly speaking, they refer to different situations. Speakers need to differentiate between the three.

Speaking extempore does not mean that the speaker has not made any preparation. He may not have made the presentation in detail. However, he does have the points of the speech ready. He is free to elaborate on each point using the words he finds appropriate.

Speaking impromptu means speaking without an earlier notice. The speaker is invited to speak on the spot. In such an event there would be no advance preparation.

Speaking spontaneously also does not offer an opportunity for preparation. The speaker speaks not on invitation but on a sudden impulse.

A public speaker is bound to come across all the three situations. On these occasions the speaker may not have made any preparation in advance. The speaker needs to draw upon his experience. An able speaker needs to be well versed with a variety of situations when he or she can be invited to speak without a notice. This requires the speaker to "think on his feet". There must be a reservoir of knowledge to fall back upon. Besides, the speaker needs to be quick witted and must understand the situation well to fit in the comments effectively.

Many speakers who appear to speak extempore even on formal occasions have really prepared and rehearsed their presentation several times before coming to deliver it. Every speaker is likely to use a different technique. Speakers who need to speak often usually "build" a presentation just as one would a prefabricated house. They have little parts and stories all ready, and assemble them as required. New combinations keep the audience thinking.

MAKING AN INTRODUCTION

Most speakers begin speaking assignments when asked to introduce or thank the guest speaker. This person can make it easy or difficult for the speaker to make a great presentation. It is customary for the organisers to request the guest speaker for a copy of his or her biodata, and pass it on to the person who is to introduce the speaker. Most people make no effort and read out the biodata word by word. This leaves the speaker no chance to complain about any inaccuracies, but it is about as flat as an open soda bottle — all water and no fizz!

A good introduction needs to be short and to the point. It must highlight the academic and other achievements of the speaker, and also why he has been invited to speak on the subject to the audience. Most biodata received from guest speakers are lengthy and flat. They need to be drastically trimmed and edited. Some people unduly inflate the accomplishments of the speaker many times even to the point of embarrassment. Appreciate the difference between praise and flattery. A speaker who is a person of honour and integrity would prefer to be introduced in the least possible words. The best compliment to a good speaker would be to spare some time to him.

A VOTE OF THANKS

Just like the introduction, the thanksgiving should be as brief as possible. The person who is requested to move a vote of thanks for the guest speaker is not expected to summarise the presentation. Nor should he comment about the views of the speaker. Even if he wishes to make a comment it should only be a positive comment. It would be appropriate if the person were to just thank the speaker for his valuable time and effort, and assure him that his suggestions or ideas have been highly appreciated by the audience.

SPEAKING 'A FEW WORDS'

Sometimes one may not be a speaker on the programme, but considering the status, position and knowledge a person may be invited to speak "a few words". A few words are literally meant to be few. These few words should be used only to convey greetings to the participants, and perhaps to put in a word in favour of the purpose of the meeting. Unfortunately, in many meetings one comes across people who present a complete "unprepared" speech in lieu of the desired "few words", much to the disgust of the organisers and the audience.

In many organisations there are people who feel a meeting is not complete without their "valuable thoughts". It is frequently seen that much time is taken up by the unimportant speakers not leaving enough time for the principal speaker who cuts down his time considering that the audience has already had enough, and is not willing for any more. It is suggested that whenever asked for "a few words" in the interests of personal goodwill one must observe self-restraint.

Think it over...

Eloquence is in the assembly, not merely in the speaker.

— *William Pitt*

THE AUDIENCE

The purpose of every speech is to convey a definite message to the audience. If the audience is not interested in the message, the presentation can fulfil no purpose. Therefore, the speaker must always be clear on what the audience wants, or does not want. An able speaker will always adjust the presentation to suit the audience. Such adjustments are not easy. If the purpose has to be achieved then adjustments are necessary. The speaker must understand this truth.

A speaker had been assigned the responsibility to speak to a group on the financial management of their independent units. Later, the audience was to adopt the budget of the organisation. The budget had already been circulated for prior consideration and discussion at unit level, if necessary. Hardly had the speaker introduced the subject that one of the audience made a remark about the budget. The speaker said he would take it up a little later. A few more passing comments on the budget followed. The principal purpose of the speaker was to get the budget adopted. Sensing the impatience of the audience about some of the items on the budget he cut short his speech and moved on to discuss the budget. He got it adopted without a change. That put the audience to rest. The speaker went on to complete the presentation to everyone's satisfaction.

A FAILED PRESENTATION

Sometimes a presentation may fail leaving the speaker discouraged. He wonders whatever could have happened. It is possible that the audience had been exposed to too much information, and it was not interested in it any more. It happens on many occasions. However, a good speaker does not look for faults in the circumstances, but within himself. The speaker would do well to analyse his own performance:

- Was I clear about the purpose of my speech?
- Was I enthusiastic about the purpose at hand?
- Was I sincere in preparing the speech?
- Was I able to speak in a language the audience would understand?
- Was I offensive and 'put off' the audience?

The answers to these questions will leave the speaker much wiser for the next presentation.

Think it over...

The clear conception, outrunning the deductions of logic, the high purpose, the firm resolve, the dauntless spirit, speaking on the tongue, beaming from the eye, informing every feature, and urging the whole man onward, right onward to his object, — this, this is eloquence; or rather it is something greater and higher than all eloquence; it is action, noble, sublime, godlike action.

— *Daniel Webster*

SPEAKING HABITS

All speakers have something to say to the audience. For this reason they are accepted as intellectually superior to the average person. This makes it necessary for speakers to adopt habits that can be identified with intellectually superior persons. These relate to personality development. Here are a few aspects that will need consideration:

- Respect for time — your own and everyone else's
- Sense of dress. One must be appropriately dressed for the occasion
- Etiquette and manners. You are being watched all the time
- A positive outlook towards life. The audience wants to hear enthusiastic and sincere people
- A complete understanding of the purpose of the speech. If you do not understand it, you have no business talking about it
- The need for research and preparation. Lack of preparation cannot be camouflaged
- An attitude of gratitude. Be grateful to the organisers for giving you an opportunity to speak to the audience.

LEARNING IS ENDLESS

No able speaker can claim that he or she has learned all that there was to learn. Learning is an endless process. All speakers love to speak, but good speakers also love to listen to other speakers. This gives them an opportunity to learn the techniques others use. It also gives them an insight into new subjects and new ideas.

Just as important as the need to keep learning something new every day is the need to keep working hard on every presentation assigned to the speaker. Success can give rise to complacency. One begins to feel that the techniques have been mastered and there is no need for extra effort. That would be a folly. No two

FRI 22.5.15

presentations are alike. Each one needs special preparation. In the interests of one's own success every speech must receive the attention it deserves.

POINTS TO PONDER

1. Respect for time is respect for the audience.
2. Reading a speech effectively is an art in itself. Learn it.
3. Without a definite purpose no speech can succeed.
4. Good public speaking skills lead one to a leadership role.
5. The most important quality of effective speakers is simplicity.
6. Diligent preparation is the backbone of an effective presentation.
7. Every speaker develops a style over a period.
8. Flexibility is essential in making a presentation.
9. Use of visual aids need as much preparation as for making a speech.
10. Introductions and thanksgiving are best short and sweet.
11. When asked to speak "a few words", a good speaker restricts it to "a few words".
12. Always respect the will of the audience as "king".
13. A failure must be used as a stepping-stone to success.
14. All speakers are identified by their style and habits.
15. There is no end to learning. Strive to enhance knowledge all the time.